65159

POLITICS

a biased guide

D0246329

THROUGH
THE
CRAP

BALI RAI

WITH ILLUSTRATIONS BY
CHRIS RIDDELL

THE INTERNATIONAL SCHOOL OF AMSTERDAM

WALKER BOOKS
AND SUBSIDIARIES
LONDON • BOSTON • SYDNEY • AUCKLAND

First published 2006 by Walker Books Ltd
87 Vauxhall Walk, London SE11 5HJ

2 4 6 8 10 9 7 5 3 1

Text © 2006 Bali Rai
Illustrations © 2006 Chris Riddell

The right of Bali Rai and Chris Riddell to be identified as author
and illustrator respectively of this work has been asserted by them
in accordance with the Copyright, Designs and Patents Act 1988

This book has been typeset in Golden Cockerel

Printed and bound in Great Britain by
Creative Print and Design (Wales), Ebbw Vale

British Library Cataloguing in Publication Data:
a catalogue record for this book
is available from the British Library

ISBN-13: 978-1-84428-778-9
ISBN-10: 1-84428-778-5

www.walkerbooks.co.uk

PART One

PART two

PART
One

To Everyone @ I.S.A,

Best wishes!

LET ME EXPLAIN...

There are going to be people who read this book and slag me off. It's not a possibility – it *will* happen. The reasons they'll give are that I've left things out, that I'm far too biased or I don't know enough about my subject. Well, I've got two words for them and the second one is "off"! This is NOT a textbook. This is not a balanced or fair guide to politics in the UK. It's a short, simply written, biased guide that reflects my own views as well as telling you how things work – and it really will!

I'm sick to death of the way politics is presented in this country. All we ever see on TV are lying politicians being asked easy questions by people they were at university with. It's always the same people talking about the same non-issues, in the same "political" language, and the majority of British people turn off straight away. There's no passion, no conviction. Face it – there's no fun. Political programmes and news shows like *Newsnight*, *Question Time* and the *Politics Show* mean very little to anyone apart from "those in the know". As a result, most ordinary people see politics as something that other people do. But that doesn't have to be the way things are. Present most people with a simple, easy-to-follow guide and I reckon they'll happily learn more.

So that's what I've tried to do. Yes, I've left things out, but who cares? Most of our newspapers sell thousands of copies in exactly the same way. And to be honest, if this guide makes politicians happy, I'll be very sad. This guide isn't for them; it's for you. And once you've read what I've written, learnt something you didn't know before you started reading, and taken in my point of view on everything from terrorism to socialism to devolution, hopefully you'll decide to dig a bit deeper, challenge some of the things I've written and find that you too have a point of view...

So while I won't make any apologies for the bias, the bad jokes and all the bloody bullet points, I hope you enjoy the book.

1 INTRODUCTION

politics: "The art of governing mankind
by deceiving them."

Benjamin Disraeli

So what exactly *is* the point of this book? I mean, most
of the people it's aimed at (YOU) couldn't give a toss,
apparently. Every day I hear so-called experts claiming
that people are bored with politics. That they couldn't
care less about voting or elections. So what am I – mad?
I must be. After all, I'm writing a book about something
that its supposed readers would rather use as toilet
paper.

Only that's not true. Back in the dark mists of time,
when I still had, in no particular order, good looks,
teeth, flowing locks and a hair-free stomach, when I
was a teenager, I *did* want to know about the world
around me. I wanted to know why politicians seem to
lie so much. Why there was so much conflict around
the globe. What *was* it that made me want to cuss every
time I saw a Conservative MP on the telly?

When I talked myself into writing this guide, I
decided I would ask a load of teenagers what they
thought about politics. I wouldn't pretend that I
understood modern young adults. Instead, with the
invaluable help of my agent, I sent out hundreds of
questionnaires to schools and colleges all over the UK.
I thought I might get one in every five sent back to me
with something close to answers. I didn't. I got *shit*loads.

In fact, I'm still trying to get through them all. They're piled up against my office wall, with my nephew balanced on top of them, like a mini-Himalayas with baby-puke stains. Here is a selection of points I've (or should that be you've) come up with so far, again in no particular order:

1. Politicians are lying wankers with bad hair, even worse suits and a strange habit of using five words when one would be enough.

For example:

Normal: "We're going to let private companies run our public health service."

Politician: "There are factors within the health service which make it imperative that we add an element of market-led initiatives, in order to better utilize scarce resources, encourage measurable performance and create a culture in which competition is seen as beneficial, with all services being consumer oriented and led ... blah blah blah blah blah blah blah!"

2. The media like to tell us half-truths and opinion wrapped up as facts. And occasionally some of the media tell outright lies.

For example:

A few days after the Hillsborough disaster,[1] in which ninety-six Liverpool FC fans died during a football match in April 1989, the *Sun* claimed the following under a big front-page headline that read "The Truth":

[1] To read more about this, go to **www.liv.ac.uk/footballindustry/hborough.html**.

* Drunken fans started the tragedy by forcing gates open and crushing fellow supporters.
* They stole from dead people laid out on the pitch.
* They assaulted ambulance staff and urinated on policemen.
* They stole cameras from press photographers.

All of this was UNTRUE and a few months later the *Sun* admitted it, but by then the damage was already done. As they say, mud sticks. Years later certain politicians and a well-known (now dead) football manager repeated these false allegations.

Or how about asylum seekers barbecuing and eating swans?[2] That wasn't true either (see **The Media and Politricks** section for more "truths").

3. You'd love to vote but aren't really interested in politics.

This one is interesting because voting and having an interest in who you vote for should go together like a Big Mac and fries. Of course, you're not alone. A lot of adults, who can vote, are the same too. The only reason I voted in the 2005 election was because my sitting MP is an arsehole and I wanted to get rid of him. The slimy, greasy git is still there, unfortunately.

[2] This was reported in the *Sun* in July 2003. To read the article, go to **www.socialistworker.co.uk** and search for the headline "Yet More Plucking Lies from the *Sun*".

4. The Iraq War is based on lies and greed, and Tony Blair is just following the USA and President George W. Bush. Er ... why?

Or to quote one fourteen-year-old lady who answered my questionnaire: "Why is Bush such a lying prick and why does Blair want to do everything the prick says?"

5. Why bother to vote? They're all the same.

Er, yes. The real choice during the last election was which of the lying, greasy, shite-suit-wearing parties you wanted to run the country. They were all promising to do the same things anyway.

* The Conservatives were going to be tough on immigration (and everything else too).
* New Labour was going to be even tougher, on MORE than everything; and it was in power, so there!
* The Liberal Democrats agreed that it was a problem and were going to deal with it fairly and with measured thought – after they'd won a landslide election victory and a (drunken) cow had jumped over the moon.

Of course, there were loads of other issues that were mentioned and I'll deal with the most popular ones later; but for now, I'm going to get on with the first part of the guide: the basics.

2 WHAT IS POLITICS ANYWAY?

I had to answer this question (without the "anyway" bit) when I was doing my politics A level. Back then mobile phones were the size of cars and had to be dragged behind you, and the Internet was a secret known only to a handful of scientists, programmers and the military. So I couldn't go online to find out. In writing this, though, I decided to see what the Web had to offer. I wish I hadn't bothered.

First of all I typed "what is politics?" into Google and clicked on a worldwide search. I got thirty-two MILLION hits. Then I thought, Hang on, I'm writing this in Britain so why do I need to know about the politics of Papua New Guinea? So I restricted my search to UK-only sites. That didn't help either. I *only* got four and half million hits the second time around. I mean, what the *hell* am I supposed to do with all those stupid pages? I would have been reading shite until I was eighty. Forget that...

Instead – and pay attention here, because I'm about to use a word that puts many people to sleep instantly – instead I turned to a BOOK. Yes, that's right, a *book*. And not just any old book. It was my own battered and scribbled-in copy of *Basic Political Concepts* by Alan Renwick and Ian Swinburn.[1] I opened it, and guess what? On the contents page was an entire chapter called "What Is Politics?" An *entire* chapter.

[1] Alan Renwick and Ian Swinburn, *Basic Political Concepts*, second edition, Hutchinson, 1987.

I turned back to my Internet search, scanning the first fifty-odd hits (UK only). There was the BBC website, another one for ITV, something by Aristotle, a closed link to a porn site called "Prime Ministers with Big Boobs" and a link to a dog called Peaches. OK, the last two are lies, but you get my point – at least, you would if I had made it. Here it is: not one of those hits told me what I wanted to know. Yet in my book I had everything I could have wished for. Feeling cheated by the Internet, I smashed my modem and set fire to the last five CDs I had bought from Amazon.

I turned to the Renwick and Swinburn book and this is part of what it said:

Politics, at its simplest, takes place wherever conflict exists about goals and the method of achieving those goals. The process of solving conflicts ... is a political process.

But what does that mean exactly? Well, let's look at the bit about "conflict", "goals" and "achieving those goals" first; and then "solving conflicts".

This country is a society in which all people live together (most of the time). But we all have different views about what needs to be done for our country to work properly. For example I think we should make the rich pay more tax than the poor. But lots of *rich* people think I'm a left-wing lunatic (I'll explain later) who should be shot, and they argue that rich people are rich because they work hard (at which point I snort and talk about the Queen). Whatever. The point is that we argue about things. Politics IS that arguing process.

So, at its basic level, politics is, well, argument. This is because we, as individuals, have our own *goals* that we want to achieve. But occasionally our ideas are different. We don't always want the same things. Or we *do* want the same things but we want to achieve them in different ways. This means *conflict*, which has to be sorted out. Sorting it out is what politics is all about.

Individuals argue about all kinds of things too. Money, property, tax, education... But if all we did was argue and not sort those arguments out, we'd still be living in caves. There would be no change – no progress. The fact that we have a political process to sort out our differences helps us to get on.

Imagine a year head at Politics High School trying to make peace between two lads who are fighting over the same girl. The year head is the political process, "solving conflicts" – like our MPs in Parliament. The two lads arguing over the girl are you and me, engaged in *politics*.

So just to recap:

POLITICS = CONFLICT OVER DIFFERING IDEAS
AND GOALS AND HOW TO ACHIEVE THEM.
THE POLITICAL PROCESS SOLVES THAT CONFLICT
TO MAKE SURE SOCIETY RUNS SMOOTHLY.

This leads us to another issue. Let's go back to Politics High. Why does the year head have power? I mean, what is it that makes him/her so special? And why should the two lads doing the fighting listen? Well, this is where it all starts to get a bit more complicated...

POWER AND AUTHORITY

Leaders have power and authority. In the UK we vote for our leaders in a general election. By voting for them we give them the authority to make decisions for us. The politicians we elect do all the "conflict solving" for us; this means we can get on with our day-to-day lives and let the big decisions be taken for us. Politics doesn't work unless certain people have power over others. This is called the social contract, and is the term used to describe the way in which we, the people, give up some of our rights to other people (politicians) so that they can run our country. In return for that power, politicians agree to be bound by certain rules and have to face elections in which we can either vote them back in or kick their little butts out.

Now, giving up our power and authority to others isn't necessarily a good thing, but at least we get to vote. Some of the other things on which politicians can base their power and authority aren't that good either, in my opinion anyway. Such as:

* *Strength*: those who are the hardest and biggest take power. Think of Attila the Hun, Hitler or Genghis Khan. Or the school bully.
* *Wealth*: rich people get all the power. Great if you're rich too; not so good if you're poor.

Examples include the United States, where you have to be a millionaire to win an election, even though according to the great American dream "any US citizen can be president". Yeah, right. Not that Britain is very different. More on that later.

* *Age and wisdom*: the old are wiser and therefore know better. (Apart from my gran, who dribbles all the time and can't remember her own name.) In Indian and Chinese traditions, to name but two, old people are highly thought of and head clans and villages, and hold power. But why should your age make you a better leader? And what happens when Alzheimer's sets in?

* *Hereditary principle*: power passed on from parent to child. Sometimes those in power claim God gives them this right (the nutters). Think of medieval and Tudor England. Nowadays there are hereditary leaders in Saudi Arabia and other Arab states, as well as elsewhere (Bhutan, Nepal and so on). Imagine Prince Charles running the country and you'll see my point. Fox-hunting and taking your plants for a walk, anyone?

If you relate this to Politics High, you have layers of power and authority. These are based on the political system of the present day – they call it democracy (see **Democracy**). The school is run by the local government, which is in turn responsible to the national government. There are rules by which a school has to be run (what it teaches, spends and so forth), and teachers enforce these rules. The year heads are employed to *run* the school and that means they have more power than the pupils because the pupils only *attend* the school. The head or principal has the most power because he or she is in charge of everyone. And it's the people in charge that make the decisions. Just like in the real world.

Or look at it this way, as a school in comparison to the political system in the UK:

SCHOOL PRINCIPAL/HEAD = PRIME MINISTER

↓

YEAR HEADS = CABINET

↓

TEACHERS = MEMBERS OF PARLIAMENT

↓

PUPILS = GENERAL POPULATION

If it's all too boring to think about, then try this:

> **Most of us ain't got no power. Some of us have. The "some" decide what the "most" have to do. End of...**[2]

Without power and authority, politics doesn't mean anything. It's just a load of meaningless drivel, like *Big Brother* contestants having a discussion. Politics means something when someone decides *what* we should do, *how* we should do it and then actually *does* something.

THE POLITICAL SPECTRUM

You know that thing where people and politicians (yes, there IS a distinction) call themselves left-wing or right-wing? Well, that's all about the political spectrum – the range of ideas and beliefs about politics. Later I'll go through the main parties and some of the smaller ones, explaining what they believe in and so on; for now, here's a quick breakdown of the political spectrum in the UK.

[2] My mate Azhar down the pub, August 2005.

The Parties

LEFT WING ←——→ CENTRE ←——→ RIGHT WING

COMMUNIST PARTIES SOCIALISTS/RESPECT OLD LABOUR/GREENS NEW LABOUR/LIBERAL DEMOCRATS CONSERVATIVES UKIP BNP

Political Ideologies

FAR LEFT ←——→ LEFT ←——→ CENTRE ←——→ RIGHT ←——→ FAR RIGHT

STALINISM COMMUNISM SOCIALISM DEMOCRATIC SOCIALISM LIBERALISM CONSERVATISM FASCISM/NAZISM

TOTALITARIANISM ANARCHISM CAPITALISM TOTALITARIANISM

Some of the traditional divisions in British politics have changed in the last twenty years and, while the diagram is as accurate as it can be, you have to bear those in mind. For example, Labour and *New* Labour, despite seeming to be the same party, are not. The original Labour Party would be seen as left-wing and centre-left. New Labour is centre going towards centre-right. There are TWO separate factions in the Labour Party, therefore: the old left and the new, Blairite[3] right. I explain all this later but it's still worth pointing out here.

You'll also see that on the ideological spectrum, totalitarianism appears on both the far left and the far right. That's because at both extremes, this type of ideology has often appeared. There is very little to choose between totalitarian regimes whether they are on the left or the right. In fact, you could turn the straight line into a circle if you wanted to, as the two extremes can be so close.

Anyway, there's more about all of this in Chapters 5 and 6.

[3] The term Blairite is used to describe the policies of New Labour under Tony Blair. Blairism, like Thatcherism in the 1980s, has been a drastic new direction in British politics, turning Britain's only mainstream left-wing party into a centre-right party – the bastards.

3 HOW DO POWER AND AUTHORITY WORK IN THE UK?

OK, if you're still reading I must be heading down the right road. Politics and the political process in the UK can sometimes be a bit confusing. Most of the time politicians think they are part of a small club of very clever people. When they explain things they get the "five words instead of one" thing going on. What this means is that when they throw words like "sovereignty", "constitution" and "Parliament" around, lots of people find it hard to follow. That doesn't make the rest of us thick, as far as I'm concerned. It just means that politicians are elitist snobs. They *expect* us to know the meaning behind these words. And if we don't know – well, who cares? Most of us haven't been to the same posh schools as them and we certainly haven't attended Oxford or Cambridge University.[1]

As you've probably worked out by now, the whole point of this guide is to tell you what the basics are, so let me explain a few things.

SOVEREIGNTY

Sovereignty is all about who makes the decisions; who has the final say in the way things are done. For Britain to work as it does, someone has to be in power. This is where Parliament and the government come in. It's the people at the top of the power tree.

[1] Aside from a few exceptions, these two universities seem to breed powerful and successful politicians. Must be something in the champagne...

But, and it's a very long-winded and slightly boring *but*, there is an argument about who is really sovereign in the UK (who has the ultimate power). Great Britain is a monarchy. That means we have, as the head of our state, a monarch – the Queen. Because we are a monarchy, a lot of people have argued that surely this means the Queen is sovereign.

However, the Queen, although she has a ceremonial role (dresses up nice, opens things, moans about having a horrible anus),[2] does not make any laws. That's left to the politicians who form the government, led by a prime minister. Because they make the laws and then make sure the laws are followed, in reality they are sovereign. So in the UK, Parliament is sovereign since this is where all the politicians do their thing.

Then again, there are many silly people who think that, because the UK is part of the European Union,[3] and this has its *own* Parliament, that makes a load of fat, balding French and German men sovereign over Britain. This could be seen as a clever argument, except for two main things:

---

[2] She was actually moaning about her "*annus horribilis*". That's "horrible year" in a dead language pretentious people use to show how clever they are (in a speech given on 24 November 1992).

[3] The European Union (EU) is a big, sprawling political union between countries in Europe. I might explain it later. If I can keep my brain from exploding.

* The people who use this argument are also fat and balding, and have prejudices about anyone who isn't British. This xenophobia, as far as I'm concerned, makes it fine to tell them that their argument stinks worse than a Frenchman's armpit.
* The UK government has a habit of telling the EU to go and stick its head up its arse whenever it tries to interfere with British politics.

Having said this, it's important to remember that the laws of the EU have precedence over UK laws; but we tend to get away with picking and choosing which EU laws we obey.

For example, if in Britain bananas, by law, must be curved and the EU law says they should be straight, then the EU wins. This precedence of EU law has upset lots of people in the UK – politicians, xenophobes, socialists, newspapers (and their owners), fishermen, little children who like to draw curvy bananas in art classes at school... Although I still think that if it came to something *really* important, like our currency, the UK government would say get stuffed. Which it did.

To summarize, then: the EU can't make our laws for us but it can tell us that our laws stink, meaning we *have* to change them – which is also the same as the EU making our laws for us, which ... er ... means that it *is* sovereign. Sometimes. See? Told you it was a wrong 'un.

Also, just as an aside, I often hear people call themselves British citizens, which winds me up more than reality TV. We are NOT citizens. Citizens belong to republics. The USA is a republic, which means it has a president as head of state and no royal family. We have a monarchy, so that makes us British SUBJECTS: subjects of the Queen. Maybe this is where part of the argument about sovereignty comes from – not that I care anyway. In the UK, exactly who is sovereign is a very boring and complicated issue which just confuses people.

So to recap:

SOVEREIGNTY LIES WITH THE PEOPLE WHO HAVE THE POWER TO MAKE THE RULES AND IMPLEMENT THEM.

CONSTITUTION

Oh great! This one is even worse than the one above. There are loads of different types of constitutions, and political thinkers are constantly bickering about them. What's the best one? Does it work? Should it be written down? And so on. But, partly because I'm lazy and mostly because I don't want to make this confusing, I'm going to concentrate on the constitutions of Britain and the USA. One is *unwritten* and the other *written*, so they make for easy comparison.

WHAT IS A CONSTITUTION?

Well, basically, the people who are sovereign over us (those that make the decisions) work according to certain rules and guidelines. Among these is, for example, the idea that they will rule on our behalf, in the best interests of the country. We give up our own right to decide for ourselves what we want to do about the big issues and leave it to our politicians (see **Power and Authority**).

A constitution is a set of rules about how a country or state should be governed. It explains the relationship between the government and the people, between Parliament and the courts, and so on. Without a constitution, politicians could just do what they liked and, as far as I can see, that would normally mean lining their own pockets, playing golf, drinking and avoiding Parliament as much as possible.

In Renwick and Swinburn:

A constitution is composed of the principles, rules and conventions by which a state is governed.

That's the definition I used when I answered an A level question entitled "What is a constitution?", and I got an A grade so it must have been pretty accurate. Obviously I had to make up another thousand words on top of that to pad out my essay. But that was easy. I just pretended I was a politician answering a simple question.

THE WRITTEN CONSTITUTION

Exactly what it says on the tin. This is a single document that outlines the powers of the state and the rights of ordinary people in relation to the state. It is also sometimes called a codified constitution. If we relate this to Politics High it would be the school rules, written down so that everybody could read them.

The US Constitution was written down after the War of Independence from Britain (1775–83) and took effect in 1789. It sets in stone the rights of US citizens and outlines exactly how these rights relate to the US government. Anyone can read it.[4]

[4] Try **www.usconstitution.net**.

THE UNWRITTEN CONSTITUTION

Not exactly what it says on the tin. This should mean a constitution that is made up of old laws, agreements and conventions, none of which are written down in one place. But it can be misleading. Again – at Politics High – it would be the school rules, only this time they wouldn't be written down. Instead the teachers and pupils would just know them anyway. They would be explained as "the way things are".

We have an unwritten constitution in Britain, according to basic political theory. But that's not entirely correct. Parts of our constitution are written down, like laws that are passed in Parliament (statute law) or judgments made by the courts (called common law). Then there is the EU and its laws, which are written down, and which apply to us (whenever our government agrees). And on top of that there are a million and one other things too, none of which fill me with any great excitement as far as this guide is concerned. A good place to look further would be *The New British Politics*, a politics textbook in which the authors say this:

> Britain's constitution is, therefore, more accurately described as partly written and wholly uncodified. It is the unplanned and unsystematic product of slow evolution.[5]

[5] Ian Budge, Ivor Crewe, David McKay and Ken Newton, *The New British Politics*, third edition, Pearson Longman, 2004, p. 89.

What they mean is this: there are bits of the British constitution that are written down and bits that aren't. But none of these bits have ever been put together into one document (they haven't been *codified*). Hence partly written but wholly uncodified. And the whole thing has taken a long time to put together, the result of hundreds of years of development.

People argue about why we don't have a single, written document like the United States. The reasons they give include:

* The countries that do have written constitutions are places where there have been great wars or serious upheaval, or both, resulting in a need to start again. Think of Germany or Japan after the Second World War. The USA developed theirs after they got rid of the British. The UK has never really had this problem so therefore there has never been any need for a written constitution.
* Britain is one of the oldest democracies in the world, so who needs to write things down? We're doing OK as we are.
* The UK constitution provides strong, stable governments; not the flimsy rubbish you get in foreign countries (hear! hear!).
* Hey, it works! If it ain't broke...
* Writing it down would be a huge task, and would you want to do it?

And so on... Like I said, if you really want to find out more (and believe me, there's a whole lot more), get researching. But the basics are simple. We have a partly unwritten constitution in the UK, which is interpreted – and often added to – by our Parliament. Which is a neat little way to get to the next point.

PARLIAMENT

This is where laws are debated and made. You know the place – Big Ben and all that. It's often called the Palace of Westminster. I'll get to how it works in the next chapter, but for now we need to consider the following points:

* Parliament, according to the constitution of the UK, is the sovereign power. It makes or un-makes laws. No government can do anything without Parliament's authority.
* However, its ability to act is limited so that it can't just do what it likes, especially when the British people object. Every politician in Parliament is elected (well, everyone in the House of Commons, which I'll explain in the next chapter) and they have to gain public support to be there. The government also needs to make sure of public support for its policies to continue. Then there is the UK's membership of organizations like the EU, which limit Parliament's powers (see the Human Rights Act 1998, for example).

* Parliament must act according to the "rule of law" too. There is a set of legal rules, a framework, limiting what Parliament and the government can do. Theoretically they must act within the law or face the consequences.

Parliament is also limited by another constitutional principle called the separation of powers. But what does this mean? According to Renwick and Swinburn:

there need to be "three arms of government": the legislature, executive and judiciary.

This is easiest to explain in the following way:

LEGISLATURE = PARLIAMENT (ALL THE LORDS, MPS AND PARTIES), WHICH CREATES LAWS

EXECUTIVE = GOVERNING PARTY, WHICH PUTS LAWS INTO PRACTICE

JUDICIARY = THE COURTS, WHICH MAKE JUDGMENTS WHEN THERE ARE DISPUTES OR IF A LAW HAS BEEN BROKEN

The separation of powers is very important because it makes sure that there is a balance of power in the UK. The three arms keep an eye on each other, so one part of government can't do as it pleases without the other

two parts agreeing. But these three arms aren't totally separate. In reality there are lots of links between each arm:

* The government can get all the MPs in its party to vote with it in Parliament.
* The government chooses the head of the judiciary, the Attorney General.
* The government, if it has a big enough majority, can ignore the rest of Parliament when passing new laws.

And then we have our old friend the EU. When Britain entered the European Union way back in 1973, it took on something called the Treaty of Rome (the basis for the European Union today) and all of the laws that went with it. In those days, the European Union was the European Community (EC), and the UK, in joining, accepted that it must obey all European laws. But didn't this take sovereignty from our Parliament and give it to the EU?

Well, there are some people who think yes and others who scream "No!"; but, in effect, it did. Britain can always pull out of the EU, but the chances of that happening are small. In *The New British Politics* it says:

membership of the EU has:
1. brought an end to Parliamentary sovereignty
2. strengthened the constitutional power of the courts.

Now, this may be strictly true, but our Parliament and previous governments *have* acted in ways that go against EU law. As I said earlier, people like Margaret Thatcher and Tony Blair have told the EU to get stuffed many times. It might all be bravado but I don't think so. The UK government is constantly falling out with its EU partners over various things; and to be honest, with Britain being one of the EU's largest economic powers, there is a bit of leeway.

Anyway, as with constitutions, this is just a start. If you want to know more, get reading.

4 PARLIAMENT: WHAT'S ALL THAT ABOUT, THEN?

The UK Parliament is the centre of political debate and action. It's a strange place, with ancient customs and weird ceremonies, but basically it's where our laws are made and debated. There are two parts to it: the House of Lords and the House of Commons.

THE HOUSE OF LORDS

Also called the upper house, this is the stranger of the two Houses in my opinion, because ordinary people don't vote for its members (or *extra*ordinary people for that matter). Until 1999, in fact, the majority of the old gits who sat dribbling through long debates were hereditary peers. In other words they were rich people who had titles like "Lord" that had been passed down through their families. So when Lord Stanley Buggered-If-I-Know Curmudgeon-Smithers[1] died, his title and his seat in the House of Lords would pass to his heir (probably called Rupert or something). There were a number of problems with this, however:

* As we saw in **Power and Authority**, the idea of hereditary rulers is a bit one-sided, really. You are born into it; so what about those who aren't?
* Only rich, posh white men (and a few women) got to be members. The make-up of the Lords

[1] He's not real...

didn't reflect society. Although that's probably why the hereditary peers wanted to protect their places.

* They knew sweet FA about the real world, most of them, unless the real world was all about drinking expensive brandy, shooting grouse and telling your butler to "Bloody well sod off, you common oik!" Not something that happens round my house.

* We all know that being rich does not make you the best person for the job. Have you seen how thick some of them are?

* Because most of the peers in the House of Lords were old and rich, they naturally supported the party that looked after their interests – the Conservatives (see **Political Parties, Voting and the Electoral System**).

WHAT DO THE LORDS DO EXACTLY?

The main function of the House of Lords is to act as a sort of checking device. When the government introduces a new law, the Lords can delay it by insisting that it is checked or changed. However:

* The Lords never delay anything that is included in the Queen's Speech at the start of a new Parliament (after a general election). This isn't a rule; it's a *convention* – an unsaid agreement that they follow. The Queen's Speech is actually written by the new government and tells

everyone what it plans to do during its time in power. The Queen just gets to read it out.

* Most governments don't change a law after the Lords rule on it. Instead they take it back to the House of Commons (see below). It then returns to the Lords, who usually pass it. So what's the point?

* In 1999 things changed. Tony Blair's government reformed the House of Lords so that an independent appointments commission would now appoint most of the people in it. Lots of old duffers lost their seats; loads of new faces arrived.

* The new faces are still appointed mainly by the prime minister, so they tend to be people who support the government. How is that democratic exactly?

* It isn't democratic is the answer. Why bother to have an unelected House at all? We get to vote for the House of Commons, so they represent *our* views. Whose views do the peers represent and why are they there?

* Then there is the mysterious Lords syndrome. Very rich individuals give donations or loans to the political parties. Then these same individuals end up being made lords. And there is, according to politicians, no link *whatsoever* between the money people give and the titles that they get. Oh really?

In my opinion, the House of Lords cannot be good for a real democracy. It's a tired, ancient institution that needs to be removed.

THE HOUSE OF COMMONS

This is often called the lower house and it's the place where our Members of Parliament (MPs) sit. There are currently 646 members split across three main parties and a few smaller ones too. We, the public, vote for all the MPs. This makes them our representatives in the power structure. We don't always get the MPs we want but at least we get a chance to vote them in or out.

I'll explain all about voting and parties in the next chapter, but for now we'll concentrate on what the MPs actually do:

* MPs debate on general matters, ask questions of the government, listen to statements on issues such as the economy, education and so forth, and often vote on laws being made.
* They work on committees that look at new laws, examining the details of any proposed changes. These are called standing committees. They also sit on select committees, which consider more general stuff, like transport or public accounts.
* All MPs run a surgery in their own area or constituency. This isn't because they are doctors. A surgery is the place where their constituents (all the voters in their area) can come and talk

to them and complain about things. The amount of times they hold a surgery is up to each individual MP. I've never seen mine, but then again he is probably in the dark somewhere, sucking the blood from a dead person.

* They are *very* hard-working people, earning about sixty grand a year for roughly two hundred to two hundred and fifty days' work.[2] Great value for money, that.

* Some of them open supermarkets and things, and some work for other companies and organizations. You'd think that earning sixty grand for working part-time would be enough, wouldn't you? Personally, I'd make them work the same hours as the rest of us, with the same holidays, and the same crap workers' rights too.

* They tend to wear awful suits.[3]

[2] I'm joking about the hard work (except for a few of them). And anyway, why should we feel sorry for them – isn't hard work what we all have to do?
[3] Admittedly this is a question of personal taste.

SOME INTERESTING BITS

WHIPS: these aren't actually whips but people who are appointed by each party to keep the rest of it in line. Before an important vote, for example, the whips go round and make sure MPs are going to support their party (something which doesn't always happen). I love the name "whips" because it sounds a bit kinky and I don't get out much.

PRIME MINISTER'S QUESTIONS: this is a weekly session where the prime minister is asked a load of pre-submitted questions by the opposition and by his own party. Most of the time the prime minister answers a completely different question to the one that has been asked, but this is normal – as are the jeers and boos. One view is that this is parliamentary theatre. Another view is that it is a bloody silly waste of time and treats voters like idiots. You can sometimes watch it on TV.

THE SPEAKER OF THE HOUSE: someone who makes sure all the MPs behave themselves during debates. I mean, why would they otherwise? They're only well educated, well paid, generally affluent adults with our future in their collective hands – I'd mess about too.

How a New Law Is Passed

New laws take *for ever* to pass through Parliament. The government usually presents them as bills, although individual MPs can introduce them too. At the first stage the new bill is presented to either the House of Lords or the House of Commons (mostly the latter).

This is how it works (or doesn't, depending on your point of view).

FIRST READING

The first formal reading of the bill in the House of Commons or Lords. In the Commons every MP might turn up to listen, although usually it's only about ten of them. It all depends on how interesting the bill is.

SECOND READING

In the Commons normally everyone has to attend the second reading, apart from a few MPs who may be ill or in hiding after they've been caught on camera paying bribe money to prostitutes and taking cocaine (allegedly).[a] If the bill is going through the Lords (which is full of old people) first, only the ones that aren't in hospital or chasing after foxes/teenagers/brandy turn up. At this stage they look at the general principles of the proposed new law.

In the House of Commons the person in charge of the new law (if it's a law about schools, then that would be the education minister, for example) introduces

---

[a] Joke ... although you might want to look at the antics of Jeffrey Archer, Jonathan Aitken and Keith Vaz – not that any of these MPs has ever taken cocaine.

its main points. Then the opposition spokesperson responds to it. After that they all vote on it, and usually the government, which has more MPs, wins. Why they can't do that at the first stage is anyone's guess.

COMMITTEE STAGE

This is a clause by clause review of the bill, going into the smallest details. Most often it's a standing committee that does this, but in some very important cases it can be the whole House.

REPORT STAGE

This is the stage at which the amended bill is reviewed in the House of Commons, through which every bill *has* to pass, no matter where it was introduced. Still with me?

THIRD READING

The bill goes to the other House, the Lords, and the whole process starts again. If at any point there is a disagreement about what's in the bill, then they have even more debates about changing it, and the thing bounces between the Houses like a kangaroo on speed. These changes or amendments can hold a bill up for even longer.

Finally, when they all agree...

ROYAL ASSENT

The bill receives royal approval and is passed into law where it is now called an Act of Parliament. The Queen doesn't actually look at the new law; her role is just a historical thing. The last monarch to refuse assent was Queen Anne in 1707. Nowadays royal assent is an empty procedure, with no real force or purpose.[5]

There you go, then. Those are the very basics about Parliament and how it works. Obviously you could go into minute detail about it all, and there are bits I've left out, but I've got the interesting parts in. Trust me – it doesn't get any more exciting.

The thing about Parliament that bothers me the most, though, is the way the two Houses are named. The "Lords" and the "Commons" seem to be old-fashioned, pompous titles to me. I would propose the following if I were in charge:

THE HOUSE OF LORDS WOULD BECOME THE HOUSE OF UNELECTED DUFFERS AND MATES OF THE PRIME MINISTER.

THE HOUSE OF UNELECTED DUFFERS & MATES OF THE PM

[5] All this messing about is a bit confusing and silly if you ask me, but if you want to check it out in more depth try **www.parliament.uk**.

THE HOUSE OF ELECTED
DUFFERS & PEOPLE IN BAD SUITS

*THE HOUSE
OF COMMONS
WOULD BECOME
THE HOUSE OF
ELECTED DUFFERS
AND PEOPLE IN
BAD SUITS.*

Seriously, though, how can it be right, in the twenty-first century, to have two Houses split along the lines of *lords* and *commoners*? Who the hell gave the lords the right to *lord* it over the commoners anyway? Not me. It's about time these outdated and discredited notions about our *supposed* places in society were changed. As far as I'm concerned, being born with a silver spoon up your bum does not make you better than anyone else, so why does the very heart of our political system encourage us to think that it does? Can't we have an unelected chamber of dinner ladies and school librarians instead? I like school librarians; they're always lovely and fair and they let you eat crisps...

Anyway, here comes the next chapter. The House of Commons is split into different parties and these parties have to fight it out at election time for our votes. But how does that work?

5 POLITICAL PARTIES, VOTING AND THE ELECTORAL SYSTEM

In this chapter I'm going to do three things, none of which I'm going to apologize for. Firstly, I'm going to give a brief outline of the three main political parties in the UK: Conservative, Labour and Liberal Democrat. For each one I'll give you a little background information, a bit of history and an idea of what they (supposedly) stand for. I'll also outline the views of some of the smaller parties too, like the Greens, the Unionists and the British National Party.

Secondly, I'm going to look at the electoral system in Britain (the way in which we vote for our MPs and our government). I'll tell you all about how the system works, why it is either great or dodgy – depending on what and who you believe – and suggest a few possible alternatives.

Thirdly – and this is where a few politicians, teachers, parents, maybe even the legal people at my publisher's, might ask me for an apology – I'm going to slag the whole bloody lot of them off. Why? Simple, really. When I was asked to do this guide, being able to have a go at politicians and their parties was my biggest motivation. I'm not going to miss that opportunity, because the political class deserves a good kicking for abusing our trust and cheating us. You may not agree with my views, but hey – that's what politics is all about.

THE CONSERVATIVES

The Conservative Party (sometimes called the Tory Party) is in trouble. Its fortunes are similar to the old dial-up Internet connection. It's a sound idea in principle, but it's slow, boring and out of date. Broadband is the way forward, yet the elders of the dial-up party refuse to see it, and that means fewer and fewer people are bothering to register for it.

It's a similar story with the Conservatives. For much of the last century, the Tories were seen as the natural party of government,[1] a belief based on the idea that the rich are better at governing than the poor; and the Tories were (and still are, in my opinion) the party of the rich. But since the huge battering they took in the 1997 general election, when Tony Blair and New Labour[2] made mincemeat of them, the Tories have lurched from one crisis to another: losing the next two general elections, getting through more leaders than a daily newspaper[3] and generally arguing with one another. The party has lost seats in the House of Commons, voters and party members. The members that *do* remain are generally old, white, posh and live in the south-east of England. But it wasn't always that way.

---

[1] An idea often quoted by the Tories, the media and political commentators. I think it's stupid. There is no "natural" party of government, and being rich does not make you a more suitable leader.
[2] Labour and New Labour are NOT the same thing, as I'll explain later.
[3] A leader is a leading article in a newspaper.

A BRIEF HISTORY

Throughout the twentieth century the Conservative Party spent more time in power than anyone else. Winston Churchill, the prime minister during the Second World War, was a Conservative. Even when he was voted out in 1945, it only took a few years for the Conservatives to regain power; and when they did, they stayed there for thirteen years. After that they lost again, to Harold Wilson and Labour. Then they won under Edward Heath in 1970, but lost once more in 1974.

In 1979 a revolution occurred. The party had replaced Edward Heath with Margaret Thatcher and she won them a landslide victory. At the same time, she encouraged a new form of Conservatism that went on to change Britain for ever. Under Thatcher, and the less memorable John Major, the Tories dominated politics for the next *eighteen* years. But why were the Thatcher years a revolution?

* She was the first female prime minister.
* She single-handedly changed her party's outlook, taking it away from the old into the new. Basically, before she came to power, the Tories didn't change much about the way the UK was run. They supported the National Health Service (NHS), which Labour had created in 1946; and left the trade unions, which were part of the Labour Party, alone. They were part of the era of consensus politics – in other words,

the main political parties in the UK broadly agreed on the big issues and only argued about the details. Thatcher took her handbag to all of that.[4]

* She introduced the idea that individualism was better than collectivism. She believed that rather than everyone pulling together for the benefit of the country (collectivism), it was much better for everyone to look after themselves and take responsibility for their own well-being (individualism). Put even more simply, she encouraged "me, me, me" not "we, we, we".

* She smashed the power of the trade unions, which were associations of working people who got together to look after their common interests. Telling the nation that they were too powerful, she began to take them apart, changing the law in many cases. Her biggest victory was over the miners' strike in the mid-1980s. The National Union of Mineworkers (NUM) was destroyed and mining in the UK was privatized.[5] Thousands of people lost their

[4] She carried her handbag everywhere. It probably held her supply of blood, the vampire witch.
[5] Mines were sold off to private companies who took all the profit and sacked most of the miners, destroying communities across the country.

jobs; even more thousands of families suffered; and many of the areas where mining was the only thing to do are still suffering today. But hey, she was a strong leader...

* She began privatization. Most of the big UK firms, the ones that provided basic services, were owned by the state – they were nationalized. These included British Telecom, British Gas, British Steel, British Rail and many others. Thatcher argued that they were too slow and wasted too much money, so she decided that they should be sold to private individuals – hence the phrase "privatization". Before they were sold, the nationalized companies put any profits they made back into the company. After they were sold, individuals took the profit and did what they liked with it. In this way the whole structure of basic services in this country changed.

* She allowed council tenants the right to buy their houses and encouraged lots more people to buy property. Under her leadership Britain became a place where the majority of people owned their own homes. If they couldn't afford to buy them, they were encouraged to borrow money to make sure that they could. In 1987, however, the price of houses began to drop. By 1989, thousands of people who had borrowed more than they could afford ended up in trouble.

For example:

A couple who bought their house for £60,000 with money borrowed from the bank (a mortgage) saw the amount of interest they had to pay on their loan go up, in some cases from six or seven per cent to nearly fifteen per cent. At the same time, their house was now only worth £40,000. This is called negative equity and it led to families breaking up, homelessness and, in some cases, suicide.

Thatcher changed lots of other things too, as well as taking Britain into many conflicts, supporting the viciously racist apartheid[6] regime in South Africa (young Tories were known to wear "Hang Nelson Mandela" badges)[7] and generally being very outspoken and right-wing. But she was a phenomenon, and a new word was coined to describe her time in power: Thatcherism. As a child, I used to sing a song called "Margaret Thatcher, the Milk Bottle Snatcher", along with lots of other people, because she took away the right to free milk in schools too, the old bag.

As I said earlier, the Conservative Party is no longer the power it once was. The party has lost the last three elections, and it doesn't look like it will win the next one either.

---

[6] Apartheid was the rule of the white minority over the black majority, with people of different colours being forced to live separately. This was legal in South Africa and Thatcher couldn't have cared less. Under her government, when the rest of the civilized world boycotted South Africa, Britain continued to support it. Shameful...

[7] Whaddya mean, you don't know who Nelson Mandela is? Get on the Internet now!

WHAT THE CONSERVATIVE PARTY STANDS FOR

* The "self" over the "whole" (individualism).
* Free trade.
* The right to own property.
* Small government: a system where private firms are left to get on with making profits and the government doesn't interfere too much.
* Low taxes for the rich:[*] they believe that rich people become rich because of their own hard work and endeavour, so why should they pay high taxes? It would only encourage them to move abroad, which would be bad for the country. Although, if they are paying sod all in tax and keeping all the profits, I can't really see how they benefit the country in the first place.
* Small Welfare State: the Welfare State is the system that includes things like the NHS, income support, disability allowance and so on. The Conservatives would love to privatize it, but they can't because the majority of Britons want to keep it the way it is. So instead they support the idea of introducing elements of privatization to it. Only New Labour and Tony Blair beat them to it.
* Lots of other stuff that I'm not going to go into.

[*] This could seem to be a controversial statement on my part, but you only need to look at the facts.

There is also a big divide in the Conservative Party over Europe. On one side you have the people who support the UK's involvement in the EU. They're called Europhiles and lots of other names. Then you have others in the *same* party who hate the idea of the EU and think that foreigners are an untrustworthy, smelly bunch. They want the UK out of the EU. They're called Europhobes and a few other things too. In the middle you've got the fence-sitters. They aren't that bothered about getting out of the EU, but then again they aren't too keen on it either. And these three groups argue with one another all the time, which doesn't help a party in crisis. Still, they get paid well.

Whether the Tories will ever regain their place at the top of British politics is doubtful. In the last three general elections they have been trounced by New Labour, and their continual infighting and back-stabbing over policies and leaders does them no good at all. But it does make me happy, as the Conservative Party stands for everything I hate. Having grown up during the Tories' "glory" years (I was eight when Thatcher took power and twenty-six when Tony Blair beat them in 1997 – I paid my dues), I cry with laughter at every misfortune that befalls them. Admittedly it's not an adult thing to do, but I couldn't give a monkey's.

I believe that Britain became a much more selfish and intolerant nation under the Tories. They were responsible for record levels of unemployment, fat cat bosses paying themselves millions while opposing a decent wage for their employees, the destruction of the trade unions, support for right-wing regimes from Augusto Pinochet in Chile to Saddam Hussein in Iraq, the introduction of a national curriculum and the demoralization of teachers, the closure of community centres, the sale of national assets to incompetent private companies, the lies and deceit over everything from the sinking of the *General Belgrano* during the Falklands War to the *supposed* anti-Britishness of immigrants, trade union leaders, peace protesters and anyone else who thought that they were doing a bad job – the list goes on.

Boy, am I glad the Conservatives voted for their new leader BEFORE I'd finished this guide. His name is David Cameron, and he's white, posh and Oxbridge-educated. But he's also young, which puts him in a minority in his party; and to the delight of Conservative supporters everywhere, he's already being called "Son of Blair", which means the following:

* He has nice, clean hair.
* He's oddly good-looking in a public-school toff kind of way.
* He's fresh-faced and young. (Did we mention that he was YOUNG before?)
* He could win the next election because the media say he can.
* He's ... er ... not Tony Blair. Well, not the 2005 version. He's more like the 1997 version – you know, the one that should have been Conservative leader but joined the wrong party.
* He's going to breathe new life into a dying party (literally, because most of its members are *so* old). And turn them into caring, sharing liberals at the same time. Repeat after me: there *is* such a thing as community ... there IS!

* He'll be photographed at some point in a pub, drinking warm beer and talking about his childhood love of football, cricket and slapping the other boys' arses with his towel in the shower at public school,[9] and generally being a normal bloke, which is what he is, honestly, if you forget about the money, privilege and education that have made him what he is.

* No one will mind that he was a director during the £1 billion collapse of ONdigital and the near bankruptcy of every English football league club. Instead, newspapers will report his time at Carlton Communications as a "successful stint as a media executive".

* He's ... er ... young. Have we already said that?

* * * * * * * * * * * * * *

All of which leads us neatly to the party I used to support...

The Labour Party

I'm going to begin with the original Labour Party before moving on to New Labour. Yes, most of the faces are the same and elements of the old party remain in the new one, but they *are* two separate parties and I'm about to show you why.

[9] That's one I made up. It's NOT true...

A BRIEF HISTORY

The Labour Party was started by the trade union movement in 1900 to represent the rights and wishes of working people in Parliament. Until it was formed, there were only two parties – the Tories and the Liberals – and they were very similar in outlook. Labour was a breakthrough for working people who previously had no voice in the corridors of power.

But this version of Labour struggled to make an impact until the general election landslide in 1945, when ordinary people and soldiers returning from the war found a natural home with a party that promised to build a welfare state. Labour's resulting period in power saw the beginnings of that welfare state, with the foundation of the National Health Service, un-employment benefits and free education for all. In *The New British Politics*, the Welfare State is described like this:

> the provision by the state of collective goods and services to its citizens: health, education, housing, income support and personal social services for children, the old, the sick, the disabled and the unemployed.

Basically the Welfare State helped those who couldn't work for various reasons, and those who needed support while they were recovering from illnesses. And it was available to all, regardless of the individual's ability to pay. It didn't matter whether you were rich or poor, old or young, black or white – the Welfare State was a safety net for *everyone*, funded by the taxes that every worker paid, for the good of the *whole* country. And it worked.

Over the next fifty or so years, poorer people made great strides in becoming educated, finding better jobs and moving into better housing. The children of working-class families began to go to university, and their children were born into the middle classes – the process of social mobility. What it meant was simple: even if you were born in a shed with no food and no clothes,[10] the Welfare State could help you to better yourself and move up the social ladder. Before it existed, poor people remained poor, and those who were born rich and privileged stayed that way. The Welfare State began to change all that, although it still has a long way to go, even today.[11]

Without the Welfare State:

* Most of us would still be living in dirty, filthy streets, dying of hunger and disease, while the rich rode by, uncaring.
* My sister would have died of cancer. The NHS saved her life.
* People born with disabilities would have much harder lives.

[10] An extreme example, I know, but you get my point.
[11] The gap between rich and poor in the UK is still far too wide and only radical change will make it any different.

* The infant mortality rate would sink back to levels usually associated with Africa.[12]
* Any person who couldn't work would not be able to buy food and pay rent.
* Easily treated medical complaints such as appendicitis and even an infected cut would lead to greater illness and death.
* Poorer people wouldn't get an education and learn about the world in the way that the rich and the privileged take for granted.
* I wouldn't be writing this guide. I'm a product of free education and deeply proud of it. It was the Welfare State that gave me many of my opportunities in life.

So, back to the Labour Party. Despite setting up the best institution this country has ever seen, Labour lost its popular vote and the Tories regained power in 1951, with the return of an aged Winston Churchill. They stayed in office until 1964, under three other prime ministers, until Harold Wilson broke their hold on government.

Then came four years of Conservative rule until Wilson regained power in 1974, and was succeeded in 1976 by James Callaghan. Then came a disaster for the Labour Party, when the very unions who started the party held it to ransom during a massive wave of strikes

[12] Not that it's acceptable to have a high infant mortality rate in Africa – it isn't. The state of Africa is a disgrace, thanks mostly to the way it was raped and pillaged of its people and wealth by European governments; but that's another book entirely.

in the winter of 1978/9. The media quickly called it the "winter of discontent" and the name stuck. The following May, Thatcher rode into Downing Street on a wave of anti-union and anti-immigration feeling. The Labour Party was in big trouble.

During the Thatcher years, the Labour Party tore itself apart. The centre of the party began to fragment, with four well-known MPs leaving to form the Social Democratic Party in 1981 (more on that later). At the same time, the far left began to infiltrate the party, and groups such as Militant appeared. These were socialist groups who wanted the party to move further to the left. As a result, the Labour Party was beaten at the next election, with the leader Michael Foot portrayed in the media as too left-wing and too old.[13] The party dropped Foot like a bad habit and Neil Kinnock took over and began to modernize the party. He didn't succeed in beating the Tories but he did make many changes, most of which helped his successors. But Kinnock also suffered from abuse by media, much of it aimed – disgracefully – at the fact that he was both red-haired and Welsh: the phrase "the Welsh windbag" was used more than once. Doesn't that make you proud of the British (or rather the English) press? Thought as much...

[13] In fact, Michael Foot was a great politician with an amazing intellect who was well respected by his fellow MPs. Also, Thatcher had to start a war to win the election (the Falklands). And much of the country supported what Foot believed in, although many people just didn't vote (as usual). The media, then and now, like to forget that there are always two sides to every story.

Next came the short-lived leadership of the last real Labour leader, John Smith. By the time of his tragic death in 1994, the party had fully modernized. It'd removed the block vote of the trade unions at the party conference (the more members they had, the more clout they had) and replaced it with a more democratic solution. The party also turned its back on Clause Four,[10] one of the foundation stones of its formation. Clause Four was the heart of the old Labour Party and its removal paved the way for the nightmare to come – New Labour.

NEW LABOUR

I'm really tempted to launch into a long rant about how much Tory Blur has done to destroy the soul of the Labour Party. But it would take far too long. So instead here's a few of the main reasons why the jug-eared Judas of Number 10 doesn't get my vote:

* He *lied* about Iraq. Full stop. End of story. I don't care whether he knew the information he had was right or wrong. He *should* have known.

[10] Clause Four called for the "common ownership of the means of production and exchange". Nationalization, in other words.

* In going to war with his mate, George W. Bush, he turned Britain into an American lackey, and made us more likely to be attacked, as the events of 7 July 2005 showed. Even Nelson Mandela said that Tony Blair had become "the US Foreign Minister".[15]

* The introduction of top-up fees and extension of student loans brought to an end the free higher education that his own generation had benefited from. He PROMISED he wouldn't do it but he did. And he's encouraged very rich individuals to fund city academies (see **Education**).

* He thinks privately owned hospitals benefit the patients they treat. Private companies exist for PROFIT. What if the operation to save poor Mrs Smith costs too much? Let her die! It'll eat into our profit.[16]

* Because of stories like the one about University Hospital of North Staffordshire, which has debts of £17 million. To reduce this debt, the government sent in a "turnaround team". This was basically a load of financial experts who suggested cutting up to a thousand jobs, most of them real posts like nurses and midwives, which are kind of important to a HOSPITAL. As a result, patient (or should that be customer?) care will suffer. In the whole of the UK, the total debt of hospitals is

[15] As quoted in *The Insider: The Private Diaries of a Scandalous Decade* by Piers Morgan, Ebury Press, 2005, p. 410.
[16] Another silly example, I know, but I like it!

estimated (for 2006) to be just over £1 billion. This might be seen as a problem, except for two things. The NHS is a national institution, so how can it be in debt? Who lent it the money? The money it receives should be spent where it's needed and to hell with the accountants. We're talking about SICK people. Secondly, £1 billion sounds like a lot, doesn't it? But compare it to the estimated £23 billion owed in tax by big business. Why can't we just get them to pay their bills and use the money to help the health service?

* He sucked up to the right-wing press and Rupert Murdoch's News International in particular (see also **The Media and Politricks**). And his advisers and ministers tried and are still trying to bully the media (like they did with the BBC over Iraq).

* Arms sales. Before New Labour came to power in 1997, they promised they would put an end to the UK's shameful record of selling weapons to anyone who had the money – including some of the most brutal regimes on earth. But once they *actually* came to power they carried on where the Conservatives had left off, beginning with the sale of aircraft, armoured cars and water cannons to Indonesia, which at the time was illegally occupying East Timor and had a nasty record of human rights abuses.[17]

[17] See *Blair's Wars* by John Kampfner, The Free Press, 2004, pp. 14–15.

There are many more reasons, but I'll leave some of them until the second part of the book. Right now, it's time to upset the Liberal Democrats.

THE LIBERAL DEMOCRATS

There were once only two political parties of any note in the UK – the Tories and the Liberals. Then the Labour Party and eventually New Labour came along to upset the apple cart, and the Liberals became the third party of British politics. Now, I could go through the entire history of the Liberals but I'd get very bored and, to be honest, so would everyone else. Instead I'll give you a very quick recent history.

A BRIEF RECENT HISTORY

The last *proper* Liberal prime minister was Herbert Henry Asquith (1908–15). That was a LONG time ago.[18] Since then they have never come close to forming an actual, *non-coalition* government.

In 1981 the "Gang of Four" Labour MPs – Roy Jenkins, Shirley Williams, William Rodgers and David Owen – left the Labour Party and formed the Social Democratic Party (SDP). Very quickly the SDP and the Liberals joined forces, ready to fight the 1983 general election. Using their imaginations to the full, they called themselves the SDP–Liberal Alliance. Even more imaginative was the quote from the Liberal leader, David Steel, before the 1983 election that the Alliance and its members

[18] David Lloyd George was also prime minister from 1916 to 1922, but this was as part of a coalition so I haven't included him. Sorry...

should "go back to [their] constituencies and prepare for government". Instead, they came third with only twenty-three MPs. A joke so funny that tribes in undiscovered parts of the Amazon rainforest *still* split their sides over it. Probably.

The SDP–Liberal Alliance eventually became the Liberal Democrats under the leadership of ex-marine Paddy Ashdown. But any hopes that he might run across the floor of the Commons and use his hand-to-hand combat skills on the Tories or Labour were quickly quashed. The Lib Dems remained the third party.[19]

In 1999 Charles Kennedy took over the party, stole voters from the Conservatives and New Labour and swept to power in 2001 with a majority of six hundred seats and the award for Rear of the Year hanging above his toilet. But then he woke up and was still the leader of the third party. Seriously, though, the Lib Dems under Charles Kennedy seemed to be the only real opposition to New Labour. The Conservatives, though they differ on details, generally see things like private investment in the NHS as something they would do too. The Lib Dems do actually have different policies to New Labour on things like tax, the Iraq War, education and, most importantly for them, electoral reform.

The Liberal Democrats believe in an open, liberal society, with a small government but one which has the

[19] Paddy Ashdown was also called "Paddy Pantsdown" by the media when it was revealed that he had been having an affair while leader of the Lib Dems. Naughty boy...

only say on tax, education and other national issues. They would abolish top-up fees in higher education, for example, raise the level of income tax for the top earners in society and provide free care for elderly people.[20]

Charles Kennedy admitted to being a pisshead in January 2006. Honestly he did...[21]

ELECTORAL REFORM AND THE LIBERAL DEMOCRATS

In every general election in the past twenty years at least, the percentage of votes that the Liberal Democrats (or whatever they were called at the time) have received has not resulted in an equal number of seats. At the 1983 election, for example, the old SDP–Liberal Alliance won 25% of the vote but only got 23 seats.[22] In 2005 they received 22% of the vote and 62 seats.[23]

Put another way, at the 2005 election there were 646 seats up for grabs in the House of Commons. Here's how those seats were shared out in more detail:

[20] See **www.libdems.org.uk** for more information on their policies.
[21] Which meant he lost his job. Not that he should have. At least he was willing to admit to being human. Good on him.
[22] These figures are taken from *The New British Politics* by Budge, Crewe, McKay and Newton.
[23] These figures are taken from **http://politics.guardian.co.uk/election2005**.

	PERCENTAGE OF VOTE	ACTUAL SEATS	PERCENTAGE OF SEATS
New Labour	35.3	356	55.1
Conservative	32.3	198	30.7
Liberal Democrat	22.1	62	9.6
Others	10.3	30	4.6

New Labour got 35% of the vote but 55% of the seats, while the Lib Dems got 22% of the vote but less than 10% of the seats. How is this fair? Well, according to the Lib Dems and lots of other people, it isn't. That's because our electoral system doesn't give out seats on the basis of proportion. Ours is called the "first past the post" system, and the Lib Dems want to change it. But they're in a bit of a catch-22. Until they become the government they haven't a hope in hell of getting what they want. But until they get what they want, they haven't a hope in hell of becoming the government. Sad, really...

There are many websites that deal with electoral reform and how different electoral systems work.[20] You might also want to check out the organization Charter 88, which campaigns for change.

On the Liberal Democrat website, their now ex-leader Charles Kennedy has posted an open letter to Tony Blair, calling for reform. In it he points out the following facts about our "democracy".

At the 2005 general election it took:

[20] Try www.libdems.org.uk/campaigns and follow the links, or www.electoral-reform.org.uk.

* 26,877 votes to elect a Labour MP
* 44,251 votes to elect a Conservative MP
* 96, 378 votes to elect a Liberal Democrat MP

Kind of says it all really. Every vote should be equal in a democracy, but it isn't. The only way for the Liberal Democrats to become a real third force in British politics is electoral reform or, in my opinion, a miracle. However, it *is* something that the so-called democracy we have desperately needs. So, even though I may have poked fun at the Lib Dems, I do believe they should be treated fairly.

* * * STOP THE PRESS! 2 * * * *

Charles Kennedy resigned as leader of the Liberal Democrats in January 2006 over the "I'm a pisshead" revelations. As yet the Lib Dems haven't decided who'll become their new leader. They'll make that choice in March 2006. But at least Kennedy had the decency to step down before this book went to print – otherwise I'd have looked a right dick. And to be honest, I'm quite sad that he's gone. So what if he liked a drink or five during the day? Even half tanked he would have done a better job than Tony Blair or Young Tony Blair (David Cameron).

Since Kennedy's resignation, a few of his fellow Liberal Democrats have decided to stand for the leadership. They include Sir Menzies (pronounced "Ming" for some stupid reason) Campbell, Mark Oaten,

Simon Hughes and some bloke with no personality called ... er ... oh yeah, Chris Huhne. However, Mark Oaten had to step down because he was having sex with a male prostitute, and Simon Hughes may not be elected because he lied about being gay.[25] At the time of writing, the party still hadn't decided who to go for, but I suspect it will be Campbell or Huhne – not that they'll win anything else.

* * * * STOP THE PRESS! 3 * * * *

Sir Menzies "Ming" Campbell is the latest person to become leader of the "no hope in hell" party. I like Ming, despite his silly nickname, and wish him well; but I can't help feeling that he isn't going to make a blind bit of difference. Can't imagine what gives me that idea...

* * * * * * * * * * * * * *

[25] And there I was thinking they were boring!

So that leaves us with the section marked **Other Parties**. Who are they and what do they believe in?

OTHER PARTIES

There are lots of smaller parties in the UK, including Plaid Cymru and the Scottish National Party. I'll deal with these two in **Devolution for Scotland and Wales**. For now I'm going to run through some of the others.

THE UNIONISTS

There are two main Unionist parties in Northern Ireland. These are the Democratic Unionist Party (DUP) and the Ulster Unionist Party (UUP). There is also the Progressive Unionist Party (PUP). But what do they stand for?

Well, the reason they are called Unionist is that they want to keep Northern Ireland as part of the United Kingdom; they want to uphold the union between the two. The problems of Northern Ireland are very complicated and would require a lot more space to describe properly than I've got here.[20] But here's a basic outline.

Northern Ireland was once part of a united Ireland. It was annexed by the English and turned into a part of the United Kingdom in 1920. Since the last century there has been a violent and bloody conflict going on over Northern Ireland. This is called "the troubles" in the UK; in much of the rest of the world, however,

[20] The Northern Ireland issue is one you can research for yourselves very easily. Try *The New British Politics* by Budge, Crewe, McKay and Newton as a starting point.

Northern Ireland is seen as a British *colony*, and the conflict is described differently. Indeed, many people believe that Britain is occupying Ireland and should leave, although you'll never hear such views in the UK media without the person voicing them being portrayed as a terrorist sympathizer or traitor.[27]

The Unionists have fought to keep Ulster (which is what they call Northern Ireland) as part of the UK. The nationalists, who want to reunite Ireland as one country, have opposed them. This conflict has had a terrorist element, with groups like the Ulster Volunteer Force (UVF), the Ulster Defence Association (UDA), the Irish Republican Army (IRA) and others engaged in violent acts. Part of the problem has been an inter-religious conflict between Unionist Protestants and nationalist Catholics. Since the late 1990s the British government has engaged all sides in a peace process which, despite its difficulties, seems to be going in the right direction.

The Unionist parties, despite individual differences, agree on the main issue of keeping Ulster as part of Britain. Visit their individual websites for more details.

THE NATIONALISTS (NORTHERN IRELAND)

There are two main nationalist parties in Northern Ireland, both of which want to see a united Ireland. The first is the Social Democratic and Labour Party (SDLP). This is a moderate party supported by many Catholic groups. Some see it as the friendly face of the nationalist movement.

[27] See **The Media and Politricks** section. This is MY opinion.

The second party is Sinn Fein, the political wing of the Irish Republican Army – a group that has waged war against British control of Northern Ireland. Although Sinn Fein and its leaders were vilified for a long time, without the consent of the party, the IRA would not have come to the peace talks which eventually led to the IRA getting rid of its weapons in 2005. Again, you can read more on each party's website.

THE GREEN PARTY

It's not hard to understand what they believe in. The Greens stand for protecting and improving the environment, reducing the use of fossil fuels and regulating industries that pollute the world with chemicals and so on.[28] They are generally on the left of British politics and have lots of other good ideas too. If only we were listening instead of burning toxic waste and using too much paper.

They have a bigger say in the European Parliament, where they have banded together with other green-issue parties from across Europe; and, judging by my questionnaire results, they may have a whole new generation of supporters waiting in the wings.
I certainly hope so.

[28] For more information see **www.greenparty.org.uk**.

RESPECT – THE UNITY COALITION

Set up by the ex-Labour MP George "the Cat" Galloway[29] in January 2004, Respect is seen as a single-issue party. That issue is the removal of British troops and British interference from Iraq. It is, much like George Galloway, a left-wing socialist party, which actually managed to win the seat for Bethnal Green in London from the sitting New Labour MP, Oona King, in 2005. In doing so, Galloway overturned a massive New Labour majority.

He and the party have been called many things, and Galloway has been investigated for alleged involvement in fraud. But there is, at the time of writing, no *actual* evidence to support the accusations against him. A colourful and remarkable man, whether you love or hate him, there is no doubt that George Galloway is one of the few remaining politicians to speak his mind without worrying what other people think. And for that, and *only* for that, I salute him.[30] Shame about the *Big Brother* appearance, though ... miaow!

[29] Galloway owes this nickname to his appearance in the 2006 *Celebrity Big Brother*. This reality TV show will make you or it will BREAK you.
[30] If you don't get the joke, type "Galloway and Saddam" into a search engine and read what comes up.

THE SOCIALIST WORKERS' PARTY

One of many small socialist parties, the Socialist Workers' Party (SWP) wants a socialist government and the renationalization of major British industries like gas, electric, water and rail. It stands for internationalism and anti-capitalism too, and the Anti-Nazi League is an offshoot. You can visit their website for an outline of what they stand for, but here are a few facts taken from the site:[31]

* Half of the world's population lives on less than $2 a day.
* 67% of the world's wealth is owned by just 2% of the population.
* The United States spends $400 billion a year on weapons.
* Yet it would take $324 billion to end extreme poverty.

I haven't included these figures because I'm an SWP member or anything; I just couldn't ignore them, that's all. It doesn't matter whether you support the SWP or not – you can't argue with the facts.

There are loads of other socialist and communist groups too, but you can check them out for yourselves.

[31] Their website can be found at **www.swp.org.uk**.

THE BRITISH NATIONAL PARTY

The British National Party (BNP) is NOT to be confused with the Scottish nationalists, or the Welsh ones either. The BNP is an openly anti-immigrant, anti-multicultural Britain party.[32] On their website they claim not to be racists but that's laughable. The BNP are a RACIST party – right-wing extremists who advocate the removal of ALL immigrants and their offspring from the UK (as well as Jewish people, gays, gypsies and anyone else who thinks that they are far-right, gay-bashing racist wankers). This would include the following people, among others:

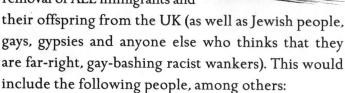

Michael Howard (former Conservative leader)
Malorie Blackman
Benjamin Zephaniah
Rio Ferdinand
Sir Trevor McDonald
Lenny Henry
Nigel Benn
Lennox Lewis
Kelly Holmes

[32] For more information about the BNP, you can look at their website, or maybe you'd like to check out **www.searchlightmagazine.com**, which has a huge archive with loads of articles that point out not only the BNP's racism but also their links to Nazi ideology and neo-Nazis across Europe.

Meera Syal
Trevor Phillips (chairman of the Commission for
   Racial Equality)
Amir Khan
the fat bloke out of *Little Britain*
Craig David
Jamelia
Stephen Fry
Will Young
Elton John
Thierry Henry
the sexy lady who presents *Popworld* on Channel 4
Konnie Huq from *Blue Peter*...
Oh, and me too

In fact, in 1998, a year before he became the BNP leader, Nick Griffin was handed a suspended sentence of two years for inciting racial hatred.[33] Part of this was his denial that the Holocaust during the Second World War ever happened.[34] What was that about not being racists?

UK INDEPENDENCE PARTY

Another single-issue party, the UK Independence Party (UKIP) wants the UK to withdraw from the European Union but also claims to have other policies about rural affairs, immigration and tax. It seemed to be gaining

[33] For a more detailed look at the party and its "respectable" leader, Nick Griffin, visit **www.yre.org.uk** and **www.stopthebnp.org.uk**.
[34] For more information, go to **www.stopthebnp.org.uk/uncovered**.

momentum before the 2005 general election but didn't get the breakthrough it thought it would, partly because Robert Kilroy-Silk, the satsuma-skinned former television host they'd recruited, left to start his own party...

VERITAS

Veritas is the Latin for "truth" (what's the Latin for "ain't got a hope in hell"?). Like the BNP but in a more expensive pair of shoes, Kilroy-Silk's party also had only one real issue: anti-immigration. Five months after he set it up, the great man resigned. And to be honest, I don't actually know what has happened to the party. But then again I only included it for its comedy value in the first place.

THE MONSTER RAVING LOONY PARTY

This is a one-joke party whose members need to be rounded up and stuffed up their leader's arse. Don't even waste your time.

There are loads of other parties but I've had enough now. Time to move on to devolution and the Scottish and Welsh assemblies...

DEVOLUTION FOR SCOTLAND AND WALES

Devolution, to put it simply, means that some regions of the United Kingdom are given separate powers and parliaments/assemblies with which they can run *some* of their own affairs. It isn't the same as giving Scotland or Wales independence, but it is seen as the next best thing. Northern Ireland has its own devolved rule.[35] Even Greater London, which has its own mayor and assembly, could be said to be devolved. Lots of other countries have a similar system, and in Britain it's been around for a long time. The Isle of Man and the Channel Islands are two examples of British devolution.

Here is how *The New British Politics* defines devolution:

> **Devolution is the delegation of powers by a state to units within its territory.**

What this means is that the Parliament at Westminster is still in control of the UK, but it has given up a few decisions to the regional parliaments in Scotland and Wales. Below is a *very* quick summary.

SCOTLAND

The Scottish Parliament was elected in May 1999, following the Scotland Act 1998 that gave devolution to the country. It has responsibility for a number of areas of Scottish life. This means some things in Scotland are different from England. Education is one of the best

[35] Another complex issue which I've only touched on.

examples. The Scottish Parliament decides all education issues in Scotland; as a result, students in Scotland don't have to pay top-up fees to go to university, so it certainly works for them.[36]

WALES

The Government of Wales Act 1998 led to the formation of the Welsh National Assembly – a Welsh parliament – and, just as in Scotland, the National Assembly has the right to decide on many issues which affect the region. These include education, culture, health, housing and social services among others. [37]

But why did Scotland and Wales get devolution? Well, part of the problem was the call for independence. The Scottish National Party (SNP) and Plaid Cymru (PC) of Wales both based their campaigns for independence on the idea that they were better placed to serve the needs of their countries than politicians in England. There were local and regional differences that weren't understood in Westminster that affected Scottish and Welsh people, and the Scots and the Welsh wanted their own say.

THE SCOTTISH NATIONAL PARTY

The Scottish National Party (SNP) has long argued that Scotland should be independent. This belief is based on the idea that Scotland would do much better

[36] For more information you can look at **www.scottish.parliament.uk**.
[37] Go to **www.wales.gov.uk** if you want a great source of information.

economically if it weren't part of the UK. And, uncommonly for nationalist parties, the SNP is left-wing too, helping it to take away traditional Labour Party supporters in Scotland. Devolution for the SNP is a step in the right direction, away from English control of Scottish affairs.[38]

PLAID CYMRU

Plaid Cymru is slightly different from the SNP. Whereas the Scottish nationalists had an argument about economics, the Welsh party was more concerned with cultural issues like teaching Welsh in schools and having Welsh road signs. Devolution has helped Plaid Cymru gain these things.[39]

But is devolution any good? Some people argue that it's a compromise away from proper independence. And Parliament in Westminster is still the main power. It gets confusing too. The Scottish Parliament and the Welsh National Assembly each has its own election, which is *different* from a general election that covers all of the UK. And in Scotland, for example, there are seventy-odd seats up for grabs at a *general* election but a whole load more when the *regional* election comes round. That's confused me so much I'm going to have a lie-down. See you in the next chapter.

Oops! I nearly forgot to tell you how general elections work!

[38] See **www.snp.org**.
[39] See **www.plaidcymru.org**.

The UK Electoral System

In as few words as possible, this is how the electoral system in the United Kingdom works:

* A general election must be held at least once every five years.
* Usually the government decides when it's going to happen – on what date and in which month, although it's almost always April or May.
* Parliament is dissolved (no, not like a fizzy sweet) and all the MPs have to go back to their constituencies and start again, trying to win enough votes to keep their seats.
* Everyone who is eligible to vote is sent a voting card. About half of them go to their polling station and vote. These votes are then counted.
* As the results come in, seats are given to different parties, depending on which ones they won or lost.
* The party that has the most seats wins the election and forms the government.
* The difference between the number of seats the new government has and all the other seats added together gives you the government majority.
* The *majority* is all-important. Without one, there is a hung parliament and no clear government. Governments need a majority to be able to work.

For example:

There were 646 seats at the 2005 general election.

New Labour won 356 seats.

All the other parties won 290 seats put together.

356 - 290 = 66 seats

New Labour's majority = 66

And that's it in a nutshell, as they say. There are, of course, lots of other little complications but the basics are that simple. Honestly...

6 POLITICAL IDEOLOGIES AND CONCEPTS OR "ISMS": SOME BASIC DEFINITIONS

Right, let's get one thing straight from the off. Defining political ideologies and concepts is a dodgy area. Somewhere in a dusty room filled with a million books and essays on political theory will be at least one gnarled old academic who has spent his/her entire life studying the difference between anarcho-communism and socioanarcho-communism.[1] In between lighting and relighting a pipe filled with cherry tobacco, this academic will probably take one look at my definitions, splutter and cough until he/she goes red in the face and then write a letter to *The Times*, telling the editor that I'm wrong and that things are far more complex than I'm making them out to be.

Well, I couldn't give a stuff. Anyone who reads this guide and then wants to devote their life to studying the complexities of "isms" is welcome. For the vast majority of us, a basic definition is what we need. Yes, there are loads of complex issues surrounding definitions of ideology but I'm not going to go into them all here (I'd rather cover my left foot in mustard and ingest it). Instead, welcome to an unapologetically basic guide.

[1] Neither of these exists. I made both up but you get my point.

IDEOLOGY

So what exactly is an ideology? All ideologies have two things in common:

* An image of society. Basically an opinion on the way a society should be. How it should look, who it should be ruled by and how that is decided on, and so forth.
* A political programme that aims to put those ideas into practice. Because what good is an image or idea of society if you can't make it real?

As I mentioned above, there are other arguments and considerations but these two will do for this guide.

DEMOCRACY

This is the big one – a buzzword that gets thrown about all the time. It's wonderful, is democracy. Well, that's what we get told in the West. And the world's sheriff, the USA, tries to export it to other, less fortunate parts of the planet. But what the hell is it all about?

The word "democracy" originated in ancient Greece, in the establishment of city states, and gives us our basic definition:

rule of the people by the people

All the citizens of a state are entitled to vote and have a say in the running of that state. At least that's the theory. But in ancient Greece not all people were citizens – like the slaves, for example – so not everyone could vote. But hey, it's a great idea!

Democracy in the above form doesn't really exist. What we have in the West is an evolved form of it, mostly described as liberal democracy. The idea of the people as sovereign exists in France and America, for example, but only as a source of legitimacy for the governments of those countries. If you recall the section **Power and Authority**, the people give up certain rights to an elected body which then runs the country or state on their behalf – like Parliament in the UK. And as I stated in that section, sometimes the legitimacy (or right) that the people give this elected body is used by the ruling classes to claim that they know best. Tony Blair's insistence on war in Iraq was an example of this. More than half the country opposed him but he was given the authority to rule by his election victory, and judged, *for us*, that war was in our best interests.

And in countries like the United States you have to be very rich or have very rich supporters even to *get* elected in the first place, which means that a vast number of the population have no realistic chance of exercising their "right" to stand for power.

But because people do give up certain rights to an elected body, in return, in a liberal democracy, they have certain guaranteed rights:

* The right to regular elections to allow them to switch rulers if the majority wish it.
* The right to vote in those elections.
* The right to freedom of speech.
* The right to live their lives free from much government interference.

There are lots more freedoms, some of them written down, as in the US Constitution, and some not, as in the UK. And part of liberal democracy also includes protection for minorities in order to make sure that the majority doesn't discriminate against them. When a majority does discriminate against minorities (as with the Jews in 1930s Germany), you no longer have a liberal democracy. Maybe someone should remind the British media of that when they begin their next round of shameful and dishonest attacks on immigrants and asylum seekers.

You have to remember too that in certain liberal democracies, at certain times, there is actual, legalized discrimination. The United States only introduced proper civil rights legislation after the upheaval of the 1960s, in order to end segregation (a policy called apartheid in South Africa at the same time). And it wasn't really that long ago that women and working people couldn't vote in the UK.

A major recent example of discrimination comes from the US 2000 presidential election. In that election the man who was proclaimed president of the United States wasn't the man who actually won the election.

George W. Bush became president based on the removal of thousands of eligible voters from the voters' roll of Florida. As most of these voters were black people, and therefore roughly ninety per cent of them would have voted for the other candidate, Al Gore, the "result" of the 2000 US election was wrong. The *official* result had Bush winning 537 more votes than Gore in Florida. But if the voters who were not allowed to vote had been given their rights, Gore and not Bush would have become president.[2]

Why were these voters removed from the list? You'll have to ask a lady called Katherine Harris, who was George W. Bush's campaign co-chairwoman, and who paid a company $4 million to carry out the task. What IS clear is that in this instance it is impossible to claim that the United States has a liberal democracy.[3]

LIBERALISM

This is one of those complex "isms" I was on about. There are so many different thinkers who have written about it and so many different arguments that you could write a whole book about it, but it would be very boring and no one except a few academics would read it (and that would only be so they could slag it off). So rather than drive myself to certain madness, I'm going to describe it as follows...

[2] These figures come from *Stupid White Men ... and Other Sorry Excuses for the State of the Nation!* by Michael Moore, Penguin Books, 2002. If you haven't read this book, you really should. Ignore what the right-wing media tell you. The facts quoted above are just that: FACTS.
[3] This makes them hypocrites for trying to export it to other countries on the back of bombs and bullets.

At the core of this ideology is the love of liberty and individual freedom, although a love of liberty also plays a part in other ideologies. And calling yourself liberal-minded is not the same as being ideologically liberal. Most people would claim that they are liberal-minded. If only it were that easy.

Modern liberalism, as an ideology, has its roots in seventeenth-century England. It began as a challenge to the established power of the aristocracy and the idea of divine rule (see **Power and Authority**). It was also a reaction against the power of the Church, which in those days was very close to the government. And it argued against the idea that people were born into their status in life (if you were king, you deserved to be king – because you were born a king and God wanted it that way. If you were born a shit-shovelling serf, however, you would never be king – you'd always be a shit-shovelling serf and God, bless Him, wanted it that way). Liberalism told people that such ideas were wrong.

The following century saw the idea of liberalism spread, during a period which became known as the Enlightenment. It led to revolutions in America and

France but sadly

not in Britain. And, for the first time, some of the principles of liberalism were written down. Eighteenth- and nineteenth-century writers such as John Locke, Tom Paine, John Stuart Mill, Jeremy Bentham and Voltaire wrote long essays on the issue, most of which you can read at your local reference library if you want. In America, the Declaration of Independence (1776) said this:

> We hold these truths to be self-evident, that all men are created equal, that they are endowed by their Creator with certain inalienable Rights, that among these are Life, Liberty, and the pursuit of Happiness. That to secure these rights, Governments are instituted among Men, deriving their just powers from the consent of the governed.

And in modern liberalism you can also find the following principles:

* The belief that the free market must be allowed to control the economy, with little or no interference from the government (see **Capitalism**).
* Respect for natural rights such as life, liberty and the right to own property.
* Removal of inequality.
* Limited government, accountable to the people.

* Universalism, in other words the idea that rights and duties are universal to all citizens.
* Religious and other tolerance.

But there are problems with this basic idea of liberalism. One of the main ones is the fact that a free market economy actually leads to inequality. So one of the basic principles of liberalism doesn't really fit in with another. But I'm not getting into that. Instead, the free market idea is also the basis of our next "ism" and that's where I'm going.

CAPITALISM

Capitalism can be described as an economic system *and* an ideology. The ideology states that a capitalist system is the best economic and political system to have. Most of the world has a version of the capitalist system. But what does it mean?

Capitalism is a system where all or most of the means of production (see below) are owned or operated by private individuals or companies. Any investment of capital (money, wealth and so on) and the production, distribution and prices of commodities (goods and services) are determined in a free market and not by the government or state. The main motive behind it is simple: PROFIT.

Means of production is just a collective term for things like businesses, factories, machinery, farms and so forth: the things that produce all of our goods and services. Profit is simply the amount of money a person or business makes after taking into consideration all the rest of their costs.

For example:

A pint of milk might cost 16p to produce. It is sold for 50p. The profit is the difference between the two – 34p in this case – although in the UK, the farmers produce the milk and supermarkets sell most of it: so guess who makes all the profit? That's right. No wonder there are fewer farmers every year. But at least British farmers are subsidized by the government and the EU. Imagine being an African or Latin American farmer. They just get shafted.

THE FREE MARKET

This is connected to capitalism and it's complicated, just like most of the other concepts and ideologies:

* A free market is one where all the buying and selling is done by private individuals and companies. There is no government involvement.
* Prices and supply are worked out within the market because it has, according to a dead man called Adam Smith, *invisible hands*. (No, I'm not joking.)
* These invisible hands control supply and demand. The more scarce a resource is, for example, the more expensive it will be.[1]

[1] You can research all of this for yourselves; I didn't pay attention when I did A level economics, which probably explains the U grade I got.

* The more competition there is, the better the market will work, and the benefits will be passed on to the consumer (you and me).
* IT DOESN'T ACTUALLY EXIST! Yep, it's just a theory, an idea that loads of people worship like it's a god. And, even if it did exist, it wouldn't work because it would only benefit the people who could be part of the market. That doesn't include babies, children, poor people, the old or the disabled.

Instead, what we have in most of the world is a refined version of the free market. In real life it is impossible for there not to be some kind of government interference in the economy. As I said in the last point above: who looks after the people who can't work for whatever reason? And if one company gets too much power and buys up all its competitors – who's going to stop it?[5]

The free market economy as it really exists is practised all over the world, in some cases on the back of great pressure from other countries. In the past three decades, for example, organizations such as the World Bank and the International Monetary Fund (IMF) have lent money to Third World countries only if they allow their economies to become accessible to companies from countries like the US and the UK.

These poor countries are also forced to remove any government interference such as protecting workers'

[5] Tesco and Asda – GRRRRRRRRR!

rights, restraints on working hours and payment to the sick, disabled or unemployed (you know, the really *communist* stuff). This is called "structural adjustment" and if this guide was about colonialism or the Third World I'd expand on this a bit more. But it isn't, so I won't. However, when you reach the **Globalization** section you'll see that the idea of the free market pokes its poisonous fingers into everything.[0]

SOCIALISM

Socialism is the ideological opposite to capitalism. In socialism the belief is that the means of production should be controlled by what are called popular collectives. This generally means that things like factories, the energy industries and transport should be owned by the entire state and run not on the basis of making profits for individuals, but for the good of the whole (everyone).

In such a system there should be no need for competition; everyone would give what they could, in terms of skills and so forth, for the good of the whole country. The popular collectives would be based around an organized working class; the main aim of

[0] Yep, you're right. I'm not a fan of the free market and its invisible hands. The market is only free for the rich and the hands have sharp claws on them.

socialism is to create a classless society, in which everyone is equal.

However, socialism in this form has never existed. The only time anything close has been attempted is in the former USSR, China and a few other countries, although by the 1980s some estimates suggested that almost one third of the world's population lived under a similar system. But that was not socialism but communism (see below).

KARL MARX

An important theorist in socialist and communist thought, Marx, along with Friedrich Engels, wrote the *Communist Manifesto* (1848), which became a guide for the left. In Marxist theory a communist society was inevitable because:

* The capitalist system and its owners – the bourgeoisie – would eventually fall into crisis because the system couldn't sustain itself.
* The working classes – the proletariat – would therefore organize and overthrow the old order.
* After the revolution there would be a period of preparing for the final end state.
* Communism would result.

This is a basic outline once again, but it works. The proletariat, according to Marx, were always in a constant struggle against the bourgeoisie and that struggle would always lead to communism. Only it didn't...

COMMUNISM

Or more accurately it did, but only to a *version* of communism.

In its basic state communism means the communal ownership of the means of production, and in that way it is similar to socialism. But the theory split into different threads at the beginning of the twentieth century, as people argued over how best to achieve the ideal state.

In Russia there was a revolution, led by supporters of two men, Lenin and Trotsky. Lenin went on to develop his own version of Marxist theory, cunningly called Leninism; and after he died the USSR was ruled by a dictator called Stalin (under Stalinism!). Neither of these two new "isms" had anything to do with Marx's idea of communism, although many right-wing commentators and politicians have claimed otherwise.[7] But you can read about that for yourselves, as this is only my opinion.

Trotsky didn't do as well as Lenin and he got an ice pick in the head for his troubles. Politics can be fatal.

In China there was a so-called communist revolution led by Mao Zedong, who established the People's Republic of China in 1949, which still exists today, although Mao would be turning in his grave if he saw the new China, which is moving towards a Western model of economics (capitalism). In setting up his People's Republic, Mao also managed to kill

[7] The lying gits.

millions of Chinese – particularly during the great famines of 1959 to 1962.

Different versions of communism were also adopted at various points in Cuba,[8] North Korea, Vietnam, Laos, Angola, Mozambique and parts of South America – Chile before the overthrow of Salvador Allende is an example (although Allende and his supporters had their own, South American-based ideology, called dependency theory). You might also want to take a look at the recent history of Chile, Brazil, Venezuela, Argentina and Bolivia where left-wing governments have prospered.

From the 1950s to the early 1990s there was a cold war between the capitalist West and the communist world. In particular the United States tried to undermine and stop communists all over the world. As a result, communism became a dirty word. It is no coincidence, then, that out of the countries mentioned above, only China and the USSR escaped being at war directly with the USA; and that's because they were nuclear powers.[9] In Chile, Salvador Allende was overthrown during a CIA-backed armed coup and replaced by a man called General Pinochet, one of the West's friends in the same way that Saddam Hussein once was.[10] Pinochet was responsible for some of the worst crimes

[8] Viva Fidel Castro!
[9] There were lots of proxy wars, though, with the US training and arming the Afghan mujahideen against the USSR in the 1980s, including a nice young chap by the name of Osama bin Laden.
[10] All of this is a matter of record. You just have to find sources. Try typing "Pinochet, CIA and Chile" into Google as a starting point.

against humanity in the latter part of the twentieth century, along with Pol Pot of Cambodia and Saddam Hussein.

In many of the communist countries of the twentieth century, the great ideals about equality actually gave way to dictatorships, totalitarianism (see below) and, in some cases, outright fascism. Stalin was a murderous dictator, for example, and the current regime in North Korea is very oppressive of its people. This move away from the ideal to the not so ideal is all about corruption and power, however, and is NOT an inevitable result of communism. As we have seen with capitalism, the pure theory has never been put into practice.

And that's about it for the really big ideologies. Now it's time for some of the more, er, *interesting* ones.

ANARCHISM

The word "anarchy" comes from Greek and roughly means "without archons" or "rulers" in proper English. Anarchists believe that the state and rulers are just not necessary and we should get rid of them. Instead everyone should look after their own actions and responsibilities and interact with each other on a voluntary basis. Individualism and freedom for human beings are at the forefront of this "ism".

But this doesn't mean that there would be chaos everywhere, oh no. Human beings, left to their own devices, without the interference of institutions like the state and government, would live together in harmony because that is our true nature.[11] All I can say is, read *Lord of the Flies* by William Golding, mate. And no, sticking pins in your nose, dying your hair bright red and puking on your grandmother at Christmas does not make you an anarchist. Nor does refusing to wash.

FASCISM

Fascism is a blight on the political landscape. Imagine waking up one morning with a pus-filled, basketball-sized boil on your arse. That's what happened to politics in the twentieth century, and the ugly head of fascism is still there, just under the surface, waiting to erupt. It is characterised by the following:

* An authoritarian outlook on life. Basically it believes in a world where all the people bow down to the power of its leaders.

[11] Obviously never been out for a beer in Leicester on a Friday night, then.

* A deep, fundamental nationalism at its core, often accompanied by racism and anti-Semitism.
* Paramilitary organizations (as in Italy under Mussolini).
* A violent opposition to liberal ideas and the glorification of war and power.
* No opposition to the ruling party or leader.

There are many other characteristics of fascism; in the Germany of the 1930s it led to the founding of Nazism, which was basically the German version of fascism. It is also an "ism" that is often used to describe the rule of the USSR during the cold war of the last century as well as that of Spain during the reign of General Franco. Many of the regimes upheld by the USA could also be called fascist. Consider Chile under Pinochet, or Iraq under Saddam. In fact, it is closely related to...

TOTALITARIANISM

A totalitarian state controls ALL aspects of life, political, economic and social. Even the private lives of people come under its watchful eye. China, Burma and North Korea are current examples.[12] The entire population of a totalitarian state is expected to support its leaders and take part in activities that promote the

[12] Depending on your point of view, you could also point to Zimbabwe and even Russia as countries where this type of state exists, although in a less rigid form.

state.[13] No opposition is allowed. Many of these states have secret police and bans on things like access to the Internet, and they actively persecute their opponents, putting them in prison or even killing them. Not very appealing, really.

And that's all of the main "isms" and ideologies, although there are some newer ones to think about. The main one, which the people who answered my questionnaire asked to be explained, is...

GLOBALIZATION

This isn't really an ideology in the way that liberalism is, but then again in some ways it could be (I told you politics is sometimes confusing). During the last century many huge, worldwide institutions were set up to promote political unity, economic development, trade and other things. These included, among others, the United Nations, the World Bank and the International Monetary Fund (IMF).

These institutions helped to bring about a great rise in international treaties, trade and cultural exchanges. By the time the new millennium dawned, there were very few nations on earth who weren't in some way interdependent on others, and this is the key to globalization. The term describes a world where countries are connected to each other and, especially in economic terms, trade is carried out across national

[13] At school, kids in North Korea have to learn songs that glorify their leader, for example. Imagine having to do that at your school: "We love our leader, Tony Blair, doo-dah, doo-dah."

borders. Just think about some of the biggest companies on earth – Coca-Cola and McDonald's for example – and the way that they seem to be present in most countries around the world. That is an example of globalization.

Another is in the area of technology. The World Wide Web is often given as an example of technological globalization, turning the world into what some people call a global village. But people generally have different views about globalization. There are those who embrace it, particularly in terms of trade (McDonald's is a major company thanks to globalization). And then there are those who hate it – anti-capitalist campaigners and poor people the world over. And here's why:

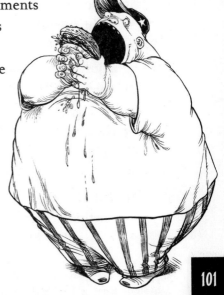

* Rich, Western governments
  want their economies
  to make money. The
  free trade ideal, where
  companies can set
  up anywhere in the
  world, helps them.
  When you've sold
  all the Big Macs you
  can to fat people in
  America and Europe,
  why not start on the
  populations of India
  and China?

* Free trade means that the rise of multinational companies (those like McDonald's that are worldwide) cannot be halted. But free trade also means that poor countries can't stop multinationals from entering their economies, making massive profits and then taking the money with them.

* Poor Third World[10] countries that do try to protect their own economies become outcasts, like Cuba, or are threatened with having their aid money removed. This is because the IMF and the World Bank control how much financial aid they receive. And because RICH countries dominate both these "global" organizations, guess who they support?

* The practice of structural adjustment is one way in which the rich exploit the poor. In order to get money for roads, medicine and schools, many poor countries are told that they have to adjust their economies to make them more competitive. This actually means that they have to let big, rich Western companies into their economies, cut the taxes they charge and stop spending money on welfare crap like education, health and preventing disease. The result is that the big companies destroy any local competition, take all the profits and no one

[10] Apparently it's not correct to call these countries "Third World"; we're supposed to say "developing countries" instead. But loads of them aren't actually developing; they are going nowhere or backwards. The term "developing world" is, for me, a barefaced lie and I refuse to use it. So there.

in the poor countries benefits (apart from the rulers and the rich). The IMF and the World Bank oversee this "aid".

* In any one minute the amount of money we *give* to the Third World is dwarfed by the amount of money that companies and governments from OUR countries *take out*. I give you one apple but my brother takes ten from you ... do the *math*, man, as certain annoying people often say. Amazingly, the world's poorest countries are paying more than $100 MILLION every day to the rich world in debt repayments.[15]

* The free trade treaties are more often than not balanced in favour of rich countries.

* Because poor countries are busily adjusting their structures, they often can't grow enough food to feed their own people. Instead they grow crops for multinationals that then fly them to Europe and the USA. The money that African farmers receive for making sure we can eat wild rocket salad in December is usually pitiful.

* Live 8 and all that other shit isn't going to do anything to solve it either. The only solution is to write off all the debts, pay reparations to the countries from which the West stole people, minerals and other wealth (mainly in Africa), and give these poorer countries a fair chance.

[15] According to the Jubilee Debt Campaign. You can find out more at **www.jubileedebtcampaign.org.uk**.

And that is only going to happen through organized political action. Perhaps all the millionaire performers at Live 8 could have a whip-round? I'm sure they could save at least one country that way – the rich, hypocritical, crocodile-tear-shedding bastards.

Obviously much of the above is blatantly biased against trade and economic globalization, and there are many people who would argue that it has been a great move forward for the "developing world", but they're just rich people who live in the West, have a vested interest in staying rich, and probably eat wild rocket salad on Christmas Day – and I don't really care about them. The facts, once again, speak for themselves, and you can find them all over the Internet.[16]

[16] Try www.globalissues.org or www.jubileedebtcampaign.org.uk for starters.

7 THE MEDIA AND POLITRICKS

The media in the UK have become more and more powerful over the last twenty years or so. That is not a suggestion. It's a *fact*.[1] Part of the media's new power lies in their ability to control the political agenda. This means that they call the shots. If a news channel or a newspaper wants to put a story high on the political map, it can. Scare stories about immigration and asylum seekers are just one example. The problem is that no one elected the media or their reporters, editors and owners. We don't get to change our media in any democratic sense like we do our government or individual MPs. So if we didn't give them the power, how come they have so much of it?

STYLE OVER SUBSTANCE

Part of the problem is that politicians in the UK have started to use media coverage in a way that didn't happen in the past. Back in the 1950s there weren't millions of shitty satellite and cable channels, all competing for news. We didn't have the Internet either. The last twenty years have seen an explosion in twenty-four-hour news and television. Because of this, politicians have begun to get all media-friendly, with stylists and public relations staff to make sure they look good all the time. Gone are the days when politicians could just say what they thought and damn the

[1] Try Chapter 16 of *Who Runs This Place?: The Anatomy of Britain in the 21st Century* by Anthony Sampson, John Murray, 2004. Brilliant!

consequences. Nowadays, say one thing that the media object to, and expect to see your mug all over the TV and newspapers for days on end.[2]

This media-friendliness is the triumph of style over substance, and I believe it is killing real politics in the UK. I don't care if my MP has a glass eye and smells like an old kipper as long as he/she can do his/her job, but that's not the way it works any more. If you don't look good in front of the camera; if you don't schmooze the right newspaper owners or editors; if you happen to have an opinion that goes against the mainstream – you're not going to get elected. I reckon many of the best politicians of the last fifty years – honest, committed people like Tony Benn,[3] the late John Smith and *even* a few Conservatives – would not win their seats nowadays because they either don't look right or have too many opinions. But isn't that the point? Isn't having an opinion something we should encourage rather than put down? I think so.

[2] Cherie Blair once said that the West should try to understand why suicide bombers do what they do. Boy, did she regret it. Talk about a media circus, and all because she made, in my opinion, a valid and important point.
[3] If you don't know who Tony Benn is – Google him.

Lovin' the Media till It Hurts

And the "Got My Head Stuck Up Your Arse" awards go to:

* Tony Blair and New Labour for shamelessly chatting up media tycoon Rupert Murdoch and his editors at the *Sun*, the *News of the World*, *The Times* and the rest. Murdoch is a Conservative and loves New Labour. Do I need to say any more?

* Tony Blair for his regular meetings with Rupert Murdoch. Before the 1997 general election in which Blair won power he was guest of honour at a huge News Corporation meeting in Australia (Murdoch's company). After the meeting, the *Sun*, the rabid Rottweiler of right-wing politics and economics, switched its support from the Conservatives to New Labour.[4] Funny that.

* The Young Labour group who had a massive party at the Palace Discotheque in Blackpool during the 1998 Labour Party Conference. It was paid for by ... BSkyB, owned by ... yep, you guessed it – Rupert Murdoch.

[4] See **www.red-star-research.org.uk/murdoch.html**.

* Gordon Brown, the New Labour chancellor, for ignoring the fact that between 1986 and 1996, Rupert Murdoch's News International Group (owners of *The Times* and the *Sun*) paid almost NO TAX on recorded profits of nearly ONE BILLION POUNDS.[5] Now *that's* love – deep, dirty, give-it-to-me-baby lurrrrrve!

* Gordon Brown once again (can you see the pattern emerging here?). Before New Labour won power in 1997, Brown frequently attacked fat cat bosses for ripping off workers and the public while paying themselves huge amounts of money. To the joy of law-abiding taxpayers all over the UK, New Labour promised to tax big business "fairly". Yet when they were asked about Murdoch and his avoidance of tax, the inverted Robin Hoods twisted and turned like eels, claiming it wasn't right to change taxation rules just to catch one person. Double-speaking, shifty Judas goats...

* David Cameron, who became leader of the Conservative Party in 2005, and immediately "found" himself all over the media, talking about his liberal views. Don't be surprised to discover in a year or two that his first meeting with a newspaper owner involved Rupert Murdoch or one of his children.

[5] As quoted on John Pilger's website **http://pilger.carlton.com/media/cultural25**.

GETTING AWAY WITH IT

And finally, the "We Got It Wrong But We Don't Care" and the "Getting Away With It" awards go to:

* The *Sun* for its sordid and dishonest reporting of the Hillsborough tragedy in 1989. Yes, it did apologize; but it was too little, too late. The damage had already been done.

* The *Sun* for its 2003 "exclusive" about "callous asylum seekers barbecuing the Queen's swans".[▯] It even alleged there was an official police report to back up its claims. But guess what? Yep, no police report, no asylum seekers and definitely no smoking, chargrilled swans – although I bet they'd taste nice.

* The *Observer* for articles claiming direct links between the 9/11 hijackers and Iraq. These reports were plain wrong. As were the reports about anthrax originating in Iraq, and Iraqi "mobile factories of mass destruction". Oh dear...

[▯] Go to **www.socialistworker.co.uk** and search for the article "Yet More Plucking Lies from the *Sun*".

* The *Daily Star* for this comment on 23 January 2004: "One in five flock here; asylum: we're too damn soft". This is a blatant lie. According to the Refugee Council and the United Nations, in the year before this headline, 2003, Britain took about 2.8% of the world's refugees.[7] Two POINT eight. That's not even close to being "one in five" – the lying bastards.

* Any newspaper or TV news programme that has ever used the phrase "illegal asylum seeker", because there is no such thing as an "illegal" asylum seeker. The UK signed the 1951 Convention Relating to the Status of Refugees. What this means is simple. In law, anyone has the RIGHT to apply for asylum in the UK. Even those fleeing to this country illegally (without papers) cannot be seen as being illegal. Imagine all the Jewish refugees who fled from Nazi Germany without papers being called illegal or bogus. In fact, Article 31 of the 1951 Act prohibits governments from penalizing refugees who use false documents.[8] Why? Because it's usually the only way they can get out of their countries.

* The *Sun* and the *News of the World* for years of articles about "tax dodgers" and "benefit-scrounging single mums" and so on. Both these *news*papers are owned by Mr Rupert Murdoch, whose UK companies manage to pay less tax

[7] Go to **www.refugeecouncil.org.uk/news/myths/myth001.htm**.
[8] You can find the 1951 Act in its entirety on the Internet.

than they should, making both papers, in effect, the bigger scroungers. Maybe they should start campaigns against themselves?

* All the journalists, newspapers and reporters who called for Piers Morgan to be sacked as the editor of the *Mirror* after the paper published "fake" photos of British soldiers torturing and dehumanizing Iraqi prisoners. The promised "proof" that the photos were faked has yet to be shown us; and the case against the soldier charged with faking the photos has been dropped, despite a massive public outcry and calls for a court martial. No actual evidence of a hoax was ever produced, yet Piers Morgan still lost his job. Love or loathe this former tabloid journalist, did he really deserve to lose his job because everyone in the media said he'd lied, even though they had no proof?

The media in this country shape the way we see and hear and read about "news". But who decides what "news" is? A bunch of unelected people, that's who. They set the agenda; they make the rules. When the drug habits of a supermodel are given front-page headlines and the latest suicide bomb attack in Iraq gets only a few lines, it's time to start worrying. Just consider this: in the last year, how many articles have you seen about the latest reality TV show or the newest pop sensation? Now compare that with the number of articles you've seen about the thousands of people dying of Aids every day or the amount of money (estimated at £23 billion)[9] that big business owes the UK in UNPAID taxes. See what I mean?

Roughly ninety per cent of the people who replied to my questionnaires said they didn't trust what the media told them. There are people who would be shocked at such an attitude. But, honestly, would *you* believe everything the media told you? Didn't think so...

[9] As quoted on John Pilger's website – go to
http://pilger.carlton.com/media/cultural26.

PART

tWO

THINGS WE'D LIKE TO KNOW ABOUT

One of the questions in my survey asked whether there was anything else that the respondents wanted to know about. Once I'd got past the idiots who'd asked why sheep have wool, and the fool who wanted to know whether I had ever picked a bunion on my right foot, I found there were a number of things that came up time and again.

In no particular order, the most frequent issues were the Iraq War, al-Qaeda and the war on terror, global warming, globalization, education, Third World debt, racism, asylum and immigration, media bias and health. When you consider that the average age of the respondents was around 14.5 years, that's not bad. It proves something I've been saying for ages – the youth of today really are interested in politics but they aren't interested in the way politics is presented to them by the mainstream parties.

So, in Part Two, I'm going to look at *some* of the issues raised and try to give brief outlines. Once again, with a completely clear conscience, I am not going to apologize for any bias. And if you don't like what I write, please feel free to come and find me in a pub somewhere in Leicester and argue with me – I'd love it!

1 THE IRAQ WAR

Not to be confused with the Gulf War of 1991 when the US, the UK and their allies went to liberate Kuwait from an Iraqi invasion, the Iraq War (ongoing as I write) is illegal and wrong. So illegal and so wrong that it can't really be defended, no matter how hard some people try. Why? Time for some more bullet points:

* If the war was to find and remove any weapons of mass destruction (WMD), then it was illegal because the UN inspectors (who were looking for the weapons) still had work to do. These *experts* didn't think there were any WMD, and there was no final resolution (permission) given by the United Nations and a majority of its members to go to war. Therefore the USA and the UK acted without the sanction of the UN – an illegal act.
* Because there were no WMD, the whole basis for war was wrong. If the US–UK alliance had evidence of WMD, we didn't see it. Why? Because, just like the mystery cat in that silly poem, it was not there...
* When it became clear that there weren't going to be any WMD, the United States made up a new reason for war: to liberate the Iraqi people from their tyrannical leader, Saddam Hussein.[1]

[1] A tyrannical leader created and supported by the West.

George W. Bush and his cronies called it "regime change" but that is also ILLEGAL. No one sovereign state (for example the UK) can forcibly remove the leader of another sovereign state (for example Iraq). But that was what Bush said he was going to do; Blair backed him; and they did it.

* In September 2002 Blair told the House of Commons and therefore the British people he had clear evidence that Saddam Hussein could launch an attack against British interests within forty-five MINUTES of giving an order. The following day the newspapers carried headlines claiming that Britain was only forty-five minutes away from doom. But the "intelligence" used came from a "dodgy dossier" (see below) and it was wrong. This claim was actually about battlefield weapons and not long-range bombs, but the government didn't tell anyone that until after the event. Blair and his mates only admitted it all during an inquiry in February 2004. Seems to me they were WRONG to do that...

* The dodgy dossier was a load of rubbish. Part of it was stolen, in some cases word for word, from a thesis published by a student on the Web. Yep, that's right. Part of the "evidence" that Tony Blair gave us for going to war was the product of a school project. What next? I'd start with the three wise men in the nativity

play – strange men from the *East* bearing gifts? Check their immigration status and chuck them in Belmarsh[2] for a few years. In fact, I'm going to write an essay on the wise men and their possible links to Iraq, and email it to Tony.

* There are only two legal reasons that allow one country to go to war with another. The first (Article 51 of the UN Charter) relates to an act of self-defence. If Saddam Hussein had kicked George W. Bush in the testicles, then Bush had the right to act. But that didn't happen. The second reason is in Article 42, which states that the UN Security Council has to authorize the use of force in order to preserve international security and peace. That didn't happen either.

I could go on and on, but you get the general drift of my argument by now, don't you? Just in case, and for those of you at the back of the class, I'll say it one more time:

THE WAR IN IRAQ WAS (AND STILL IS)
ILLEGAL.
WRONG.
BOGUS.

[2] See **War on Terror**. Belmarsh Prison is Britain's Guantánamo Bay.

SOME INTERESTING FACTS ABOUT SADDAM HUSSEIN, IRAQ, THE USA AND THE UK

* Iraq as we know it came into existence as a British colony at the end of the First World War. Before this it was not a country. It was granted independence from British rule in 1932.[3]

* In 1968 the Ba'ath Party overthrew President Rahman Arif. In 1979 Saddam Hussein assumed control of the party and the presidency, killing off his opponents. During a speech to the Ba'ath Party, which Saddam had recorded, he ordered the executions, on the spot, of several of his key opponents. He was obviously *not* a very nice man.

* In 1979 a revolutionary Islamic movement overthrew the ruler of neighbouring Iran, the shah. The shah was a close ally of the British and the Americans, and they were not happy. In September 1980 Iraq invaded Iran. The US and the UK were a bit happier and supported Saddam Hussein in his aims.

* From 1982 to 1988 the US government provided Iraq with intelligence about Iranian positions and supplied weapons too. The US and UK saw Islamic Iran as a threat to their interests in the Middle East and used Saddam Hussein to try to get rid of that threat. The duplicitous, conniving ... er ... gits!

[3] This is HISTORY!

* In November 1983 the US Secretary of State, George Schultz, was informed that Iraq was using chemical weapons against Iranian soldiers on a daily basis. In December 1983 – the FOLLOWING month – Donald Rumsfeld, now one of the most anti-Saddam politicians in the United States, met Saddam in Baghdad, assuring him of US support and friendship.[4]

* The UK government at the time, led by Margaret Thatcher, gave Saddam £340 million in export credits (like a credit note from a shop, paid for by British taxpayers).[5] In fact, British companies, as well as companies from the United States, Germany, Austria and other countries, supplied Saddam and Iraq with weapons and equipment throughout the 1980s – even though it was illegal to do so. And every company had government support. The case over Matrix-Churchill and the Scott Inquiry of 1993 prove that the UK government was supporting Saddam.[6]

* Saddam Hussein used chemical weapons against Kurdish Iraqis in 1988. At Halabja, five thousand villagers were killed. There are

[4] See **www.iranchamber.com/history** or **www.gwu.edu** (search for the Iran–Iraq War), or even **www.greenleft.org.au**. Alternatively you could try typing "who armed Saddam" into Google. Happy hunting...
[5] As quoted in John Pilger's article "Lies, Damned Lies and Terror Warnings", in the *Mirror*, 3 December 2002. Go to **www.mirror.co.uk** and search for this article.
[6] From *Blair's Wars* by John Kampfner, The Free Press, 2003, pp. 7–8. Or just search the Internet for "Scott Inquiry and Matrix-Churchill".

many who believe that Bell helicopters, designed for crop spraying, were used in the attack.[7] Guess which country supplied them?

* On 9 February 1994 Senator Donald W. Riegle said the following in the US Senate (like our House of Commons):[8]

Between ... 1985 and 1989, the United States government approved the sales of ... potentially lethal *biological* agents that could have been cultured and grown in very large quantities in an Iraqi biological warfare programme...

Anthrax was shipped from the United States to Iraq ... on 2 May 1986, and again in September 1988... *Clostridium botulinum* ... on 22 May 1986, and again in September 1988 ... several shipments of *E. coli* and genetic materials, *human* and bacterial DNA, were shipped directly to the Iraq Atomic Energy Commission...

We *know* we sent the stuff. We *know* our Government approved it [my italics].

Was Senator Riegle thrown into prison for lying? Er ... no. He was telling the truth. No wonder George W. Bush was so adamant that Saddam had chemical and

[7] See **www.greenleft.org.au**.
[8] You can read Senator Riegle's speech at
http://pubs.socialistreview.org.uk/sr267/morgan1.htm.

biological weapons. He was the new owner of the shop that had sold them to him.

So, to recap, when the US–UK coalition failed to find weapons of mass destruction, they decided to tell the world that Saddam was an evil bastard who had used chemicals and gas on his own people. They said that this was yet another reason to remove him from power. But it was the United States and the UK and other Western governments that had given him the weapons and let him use them. Saddam Hussein was the West's gimp. There's a word for all of the above and that word is:

HYPOCRISY!

They also tried to link Saddam to the 9/11 attacks on New York and Washington and to international terrorism (al-Qaeda) before invading Iraq in 2003. I'll let you make up your own minds about whether those accusations were true or not...

2 THE WAR ON TERROR

Hmm... According to Bush and Blair, the war on terror is being fought against terrorists and the nations that harbour them. So why not call it "war against terrorists and the nations that harbour them"? Just not catchy enough, is it? I mean, imagine fitting that across a TV screen. Better to call it something simple, catchy, quick. That'll get the public worrying...

Other than silly arguments about what to call it, the main problem with fighting a war against "rogue" states and countries *harbouring* or *training* terrorists is that it all depends on your definition of who or what a terrorist is.

Osama bin Laden is definitely a terrorist. We don't need to be told this. But wasn't he trained and supported by the Central Intelligence Agency (CIA), the US secret service?[1] And if that's true, then should the United States be fighting against itself?

According to George Monbiot in the *Guardian*, the United States has for the past fifty-odd years been running a terrorist training camp. The Western Hemisphere Institute for Security Cooperation (WHISC) is based in Fort Benning, Georgia, and is funded by the US government.[2]

---

[1] Try checking out CIA and US involvement in the war between Afghanistan and the USSR that started in 1979. The US trained, armed and supported Islamic rebels, the mujahideen, against the Russians. Guess who was a major player in the mujahideen? Osama bin Laden...

[2] George Monbiot, "America's Terrorist Training Camp", in the *Guardian*, 30 October 2001. You can read the whole article on his website at **www.monbiot.com**.

When I was doing my degree, part of which was in Latin American politics, WHISC was called "the School of the Americas" (SOA). Therefore I know that Mr Monbiot is not telling porkies. Some of the worst torturers, thugs and mercenaries in Latin America (and there are a lot) were trained at SOA – sixty thousand of them since 1946, according to Monbiot and the pressure group SOA Watch. Like Colonel Byron Lima Estrada, for example, an ex-student of SOA, who was convicted of killing a bishop (Juan Gerardi) in Guatemala in 1998. Bishop Gerardi had reported on how Lima Estrada ran a military intelligence group called D-2 which murdered tens of thousands of Mayan villagers.[3]

Or like General Leopoldo Galtieri, head of the Argentine junta that lost the Falklands War against the UK. He was responsible for the deaths or disappearances of thousands of people. And he was trained by the USA at the SOA. Hmm... Or even Carlos Medina Caray, who was identified by a United Nations report into war atrocities in El Salvador during the 1980s. Caray took part in the 1981 El Junquillo massacre in which troops raped and murdered children, some as young as twelve. Guess where he went to school?[4]

All of which begs the question: *as it is also training and harbouring terrorists,* will the US bomb itself too?

---

[3] Also mentioned in Monbiot's "America's Terrorist Training Camp" article.
[4] See **www.socialistworker.co.uk** (search for the article "The Terror Unleashed by the US") or **www.thirdworldtraveler.com/Terrorism/SOA.html**. Or you could try the Amnesty International and Human Rights Watch websites (**www.amnesty.org** and **www.hrw.org**).

And what about your definition of terrorism itself? Does it apply equally to ALL countries or can you pick and choose? Well, the US and Britain generally like to pick and choose. Just compare the human rights records of Iraq (which they bombed) and Saudi Arabia (which they love). Compare women's rights in China (we love you, long time) to those in Afghanistan (we're going to bomb you back into the Dark Ages).

Not to mention that terrorism is not just about suicide bombers and kidnappings. The coalition of the US and the UK and other countries dropped more bombs on Afghanistan and Iraq than either of those countries ever dropped on anyone else. One of these bombs – called the daisy cutter – is a weapon of mass destruction weighing fifteen thousand pounds that carpet-bombs the area it is dropped on. So you hit your target but then it carries on and hits schools, hospitals and occasionally a wedding party. Now imagine that you are a schoolchild in Afghanistan sitting in class, trying to recite your times tables. You hear a thundering, rumbling sound, so loud that it feels as though every thundercloud in the world is above your head. You run for the window; explosions are going off all around. First one huge one, then another, then another. Everywhere people are screaming, dying. *You* scream; you run. You are terrified. TERRORIZED. Who's the terrorist now?

So Why Did the War on Terror Start?

On 11 September 2001 suicide bombers attacked the United States, using planes to crash into the World Trade Center, the Pentagon and a field in Pennsylvania. Around three thousand innocent people were murdered. The plane hijackers were supporters of Osama bin Laden and a shadowy organization that the US started calling al-Qaeda. It very quickly became clear that it was a terrorist attack.[5]

Within days the US government was pointing the finger not just at bin Laden, but also at Afghanistan for hiding him and, incredibly, at Iraq and Saddam Hussein, who had absolutely NO LINK WHATSOEVER with the attacks. In fact, nearly all the terrorists involved in 9/11 were from Saudi Arabia, long-time ally of the US and the West and supplier of OIL. That old "black gold"[6] can help excuse a lot, can't it? By the following month, the US, with support from the UK among others, started to bomb Afghanistan to remove the Taliban regime that ran the country. Bin Laden and his cronies escaped. As did Mullah Omar, the one-eyed, crippled leader of the Taliban, who got away on a *motorbike*.

The US–UK alliance then turned its attentions to Iraq. While much of the world supported action against Afghanistan because bin Laden was hiding there, they *didn't* support the action against Iraq, which had nothing to do with the 9/11 attacks. At the same time, secret services in countries around the Western

[5] Although if this is the first you've heard of it, please put this book down and go and boil your head.
[6] Black gold is another term for oil. If you've got it, you're minted.

world began to keep tabs on suspected terrorists and leaders, as well as a few completely innocent people who just happened to be called Akhbar or Mohammed.

The Iraq War began in March 2003. By 1 May that same year, Bush declared it was over. He was lying. The war is still ongoing as I write.

The Americans captured lots of prisoners, both in Afghanistan and Iraq. But they decided they wouldn't call them prisoners of war because that would mean they were protected by the Geneva Convention.[7] Instead Bush and his mates started calling them enemy combatants and took them to prisons like Guantánamo Bay in Cuba, where they were held without charge, representation by lawyers or trial for as long as the United States wanted.

Enemy combatants ARE prisoners of war. If they are the enemy then they *must* be fighting in the war. If they are combatants, then they *must* be fighters. When you capture enemy fighters during a war, they are *prisoners* of that war. Which makes them PRISONERS OF WAR. Er ... not according to the United States. They were so *not* prisoners of war protected by the Geneva Convention that in April and May 2004 photographs appeared of naked Iraqi "combatants" being sexually and physically abused and tortured in Abu Ghraib Prison. In each photograph a smiling US soldier could be seen. The face of a just and moral cause to liberate the Iraqi people?

[7] See **www.genevaconventions.org** for more details.

The UK and the War on Terror

OK, so far so good, but what does the war on terror mean for the United Kingdom? Well, quite a lot actually. Not only did the UK's involvement with George W. Bush make us more likely to be attacked ourselves, but it also led to some quite serious changes in UK laws, and strengthened the powers of the security services, which is scary when you consider how shady or secret those "services" actually are and the fact that, as ordinary British subjects, we have no control over them at all.

Here are a few points about the UK's role in the war on terror.

Belmarsh Prison

Belmarsh Prison is in London, and after the 9/11 attacks in 2001 it held terror suspects without charge or trial. In December 2001 nine foreign nationals were arrested and taken to Belmarsh, and they were still there in June 2004, according to Denise Winterman of the BBC.[] None of them were charged with a crime or told why they were there; on top of that, they were locked in their cells for twenty-two hours a day. This is how Amnesty International condemned the British government over Belmarsh:

> **We have heard reports of inadequate health care, restricted access to legal advice, to the outside world and to**

[] "Belmarsh – Britain's Guantánamo Bay?" by Denise Winterman, 6 October 2004. To read this article go to **http://news.bbc.co.uk**.

practising their religion. The conditions
are cruel, inhuman and degrading. The
parallels with Guantánamo Bay are
stark.[9]

The civil liberties group Liberty agreed, in the same article, that:

The lack of rights afforded to the men
in both places undermines fundamental
civil liberties.

Amnesty International is well known for its work against cruel, inhuman and unjust regimes all over the world. Personally, the fact that they found the UK's record on terror suspects appalling makes me feel ashamed. These people, most of whom were freed on strict bail conditions during 2005, were suspects. They were not charged, tried or convicted of any crime yet they were made to disappear. It's like something out of *Nineteen Eighty-Four* by George Orwell.[10] Even the Law Lords, who rule on issues such as detention without trial, called the treatment of Belmarsh detainees "unlawful". Eight out of nine of them to be precise.[11] And it was legal challenges that led to them being freed on bail – not a sudden attack of conscience at Number 10.

[9] Quoted in Winterman's article "Belmarsh – Britain's Guantánamo Bay?"
[10] It's a book. Read it.
[11] "The End of Belmarsh" by Louise Christian, published in the *Guardian* on 17 December 2004; you can read this article on **www.guardian.co.uk**.

Of course, none of the above would have been possible without...

THE ANTI-TERRORISM, CRIME AND SECURITY ACT 2001

This was an emergency piece of legislation rushed into law after the 9/11 attacks in America. It was heavily opposed at the time, mainly because critics argued that much of it would do little or nothing to stop potential attacks on the UK. In fact, parts of it were originally dropped from the Terrorism Act 2000 because our elected officials (MPs) objected to them.

The Anti-Terrorism, Crime and Security Act 2001 (ATCSA) allowed, among other things:

* The detention of non-British citizens believed by the home secretary to be terrorists.
* The detention of people whose presence in the UK might be a threat to national security.
* The prosecution of the detained individuals if there was enough evidence.
* The deportation of the detained individuals using the Immigration Act 1971 if there was not enough or no evidence.

But after a ruling by the European Court of Human Rights, deportation was not allowed to countries where the detainees might be subject to torture or inhuman or degrading treatment.[12]

[12] They got enough of that at Belmarsh anyway.

So the government decided the following (pay close attention): there were foreigners in the UK who they *believed* were terrorists, but couldn't prosecute because there wasn't enough evidence (or any evidence at all). But at the same time, these people were *believed* to pose a threat to national security, only they couldn't be deported because they might get tortured in whichever country they were deported to. And no other country was willing to take them. Still with me? So therefore the only solution was to hold these "suspects" indefinitely, without charge or trial, until they no longer posed a threat to national security or some other country decided to have them.

Or put it this way. You live in my house. Not as part of my family – you're just a rent-paying lodger. I *suspect* that you have been using my toothbrush to clean the toilet but I have no proof. Only I don't need proof because I *believe* that you are doing it and, because it's MY house, that's enough. But I can't just turf you out – you might get beaten up in some other house because you look a bit shifty. So, because I can't get rid of you and there's no proof that you're the one cleaning the toilet with my toothbrush, the best thing all round is for me to lock you in your room until any thoughts that you might have about using my toothbrush as a bog-cleaning implement have left your brain. There – does that make it clearer?

Or ... I've no proof that you've done anything wrong, but I've got my suspicions. No one else will have you. I know – I'll lock you in a cell. Just in case you are thinking of doing something. *Minority Report*, anyone?

Now, if all this sounds a bit crazy to you, don't worry. It would to anyone with any sense of morality. On the other hand, if you think they are perfectly reasonable laws, you're entitled to your opinion but please put this book down. NOW!

The ATCSA 2001 was updated in 2005 and led to yet more controversy. In it, the government decided it wanted to increase the powers it gave itself in 2001. This included:

* Plans to allow police to detain terror suspects for up to ninety days without charge (it was supposed to be fourteen days).[13]
* A new offence of "glorification or indirect incitement of terrorism". In other words, it becomes an offence to encourage terrorism or terrorist acts, to say you support them or to promote them via articles, websites and so forth.

As I was writing this, the government's 2005 Terrorism Bill was defeated in the House of Commons. The ninety-day detention without trial period was reduced to twenty-eight days, for example, as forty-nine Labour MPs voted against their own government. It had yet to pass into law, however.[14]

[13] But at least it's a step forward from Belmarsh.
[14] If you're interested, you can read all about it at **www.publications.parliament.uk**.

7 JULY 2005

Despite all the new powers given to the police and the security services, London was attacked on 7 July 2005. Four suicide bombers blew themselves and innocent people up on three Underground trains and a bus. Fifty-two people died and seven hundred were injured. All of the bombers were identified as young British men. In the weeks that followed, many commentators and politicians argued about the bombings.

* One side of the debate took the government's view that the UK was always going to be a target, which is why we needed such strong anti-terrorism laws.
* The other side argued that before the UK joined the United States in its war on terror, Britain was not a target at all. It was the UK's involvement in Iraq that led to the 7 July bombs.[16]

It is hard to say for certain which side of the argument is correct, but it IS important to have a point of view. In my opinion the bombings were a direct consequence of Tony Blair's illegal invasion of Iraq. The Muslim world saw the war on terror as a war against Islam. This was partly to do with the hypocrisy surrounding the reasons for war with Iraq. Why was Iraq attacked, when:

[16] Spain was another major European country to join the US-led coalition in Iraq. It was also bombed.

- * It had nothing to do with 9/11 or any other al-Qaeda acts?
- * It had no weapons of mass destruction, unlike many other countries?
- * It had been left alone after the end of the 1991 Gulf War, when it actually broke international law?
- * Israel continually breaks United Nations resolutions over its illegal occupation of Palestinian land yet suffers no sanctions from the West?[16]

The lack of a fair response to the problems of the Middle East and what seem to Muslims to be indiscriminate and illegal attacks on Islam have led to more extremism in the world, not less. The war on terror has just led to more terror, and when you consider the human rights abuses carried out by the British and the Americans in Guantánamo Bay, Belmarsh, Abu Ghraib and elsewhere, and the US forces' use of chemical weapons against Iraqis,[17] alongside America's arming of Saddam Hussein in the first place, you can begin to understand a little bit better why so many young Muslims are pissed off with the West.

However, to say that I *understand* Muslim anger is *not the same* as saying that I agree with or condone suicide bombing or any other terrorist act. I don't at all. But as I stated in the section about Afghanistan and

[16] Over thirty UN resolutions have been ignored by Israel, one of the biggest reasons for anti-Western feeling in the Muslim world.
[17] See the article "US used White Phosphorus in Iraq", published on 16 November 2005, at **http://news.bbc.co.uk**.

carpet bombs, sometimes it's hard to tell one terrorist from another. Personally, I don't see the difference between dropping bombs from the sky and blowing yourself and others up. When innocent people die, then IT'S ALL WRONG.

Time to move on...

3 GLOBAL WARMING

There are two arguments about global warming. One says that it is definitely happening and is a massive threat to the future of the earth. The second claims that it isn't happening, at least not too much, and the threat is being exaggerated by scientists and smelly, hairy people who like to eat vegetables. Because of this, many facts about global warming are hotly disputed. I typed "global warming facts" into a search engine and got completely confused.

The first hit I clicked on took me to a site called Global Warming.[1] This site, which sounded to me as though it would support claims that global warming exists, is actually the complete opposite. According to its home page, there is no such thing as global warming. But then again, this site is also heavily biased towards the US government, and claims that attempts to stop greenhouse gases such as the Kyoto Treaty[2] are bad for business. Considering that America uses twenty-five per cent of ALL the world's resources and is one of the biggest polluters on earth, it would say that, wouldn't it?

The second site I checked out was the good old BBC, and they have a different take.[3] With graphics showing the earth, sea levels, crop patterns and various other things, the BBC website lists a number of reasons why global warming may be occurring.

[1] At **www.globalwarming.org**.
[2] Oh, Google it, you lazy shits...
[3] See **www.bbc.co.uk**.

It really is a great place to look if you're interested. In fact, it's probably a good idea to compare the two sites I've just mentioned. As well as being fair and balanced.

BUT as I have stated throughout this book: fair and balanced are boring and this isn't a textbook. From the things I've read it seems obvious to me that global warming IS happening. You only have to look at the fact that the polar ice caps are beginning to melt to understand that our world is polluted beyond repair. Warmer winters and hotter summers are now a matter of record, and severe or strange weather patterns are occurring from Mozambique to Bangladesh and Portugal, not to mention Siberia, Scandinavia and Britain. I mean, since when did we have floods on such a regular basis? Sea levels have also risen. That is a fact. But don't take my word for it. Try the following organizations, all of whom agree with me: Greenpeace, Friends of the Earth, Oxfam, the US Environmental Protection Agency (see below), the World Wildlife Fund, the World Health Organization. There are more too, but listing them would stop me from writing the following...

THE US GOVERNMENT AND THE CENSORED REPORT

In 2003 the US government censored a report by one of its *own* agencies. The report by the Environmental Protection Agency (EPA) contradicted what George W. Bush and his cronies were saying about climate change. It bothered them so much that they butchered it. For example, part of the original version of the report stated that:

Climate change has global consequences for human health and the environment.

Doesn't get much clearer, does it? Only Bush and his mates didn't like it – maybe it was too easy to understand. So they replaced it with:

The complexity of the Earth system and the interconnections among its components make it a scientific challenge to document change, diagnose its causes and develop useful projections of how natural variability and human actions may affect the global environment in the future.[a]

So that's cleared that up, then...

What you have to remember about Bush and other opponents of the global warming "conspiracy" is that they are in bed with the energy industry. Bush got lots of the money he used to become president from oil and other energy companies. His family are in the oil business and his country is the biggest user of energy

[a] As quoted in Duncan Campbell's article "White House Cuts Global Warming from Report", in the *Guardian*, 20 June 2003. Read the article in full at **www.guardian.co.uk**. Also see my comment in the **Introduction** about lying politicians and their doublespeak.

on the planet. He's hardly likely to have a go at the companies that made him, is he? No, he isn't. Now, I may be biased, but I don't have an entire oil industry to arse-lick. And nor do Greenpeace and the rest of them. So tell me, given the choice – who you gonna love?

4 EDUCATION

Well, what can I say? Quite a lot, actually:

* For a start there are faith schools. Now, I'm not talking about places where they take pupils no matter what their background, but real, single-faith institutions that make me want to puke. What a great way to encourage harmony among our children. Keep them separated ... yep, that'll work. A particular favourite of the Reverend Tony Blair, these. And a sure-fire way to create even more divided communities.

* Or the city academies, which are privatized schools. Yes, that's what I said. Privatized in that private individuals, for a donation of about £2 million, get to run them. The rest of the money comes from the taxpayer – just like with the "privatized" rail services.[1] These schools are well-run places, like the one I visited where the whole of Year Nine was sent out to the cinema because some posh visitors were coming round. Yes, the ENTIRE Year Nine. Buses laid on and everything.[2]

* How about LEA outsourcing, which is a posh name for privatizing the Local Education

[1] Oi, Blair! If it uses taxpayers' money then it's NOT REALLY PRIVATE, IS IT? Back of the class, you oily git!
[2] Brilliant teachers, brilliant kids; stupid, useless managers and a useless building. Welcome to the school of the future...

Authority (LEA)? This happened in Bradford in 2001 with the LEA being rebranded as Education Bradford by its new owners, a company called Serco, on a £360 million contract over ten years. According to John Harris in his brilliant book *So Now Who Do We Vote For?*,[3] Serco also ran HM Prison Dover, the Docklands Light Railway and hundreds of speed cameras at the time. So why not try education? It's *easy*, innit? We'll just combine all of our businesses into one! We'll run the pupils along tracks so that they can't miss classes. Those that do miss classes (because the train tracks failed due to leaves on the line) will be flashed by our speed – I mean *school* – cameras. And the little bastards that don't get us enough Ofsted points – we'll just chuck them in prison. Easy...

* Or the schools in the north-east that are run by the Vardy Foundation? A group of Christian fundamentalists who want to teach creationism (Adam and Eve, pay attention!) alongside evolution in biology. What next – telling pupils that homosexuality is "against God's design"? Oh no, wait a minute, Nigel McQuoid, head of the Vardy Foundation's King's Academy in Middlesbrough, DID say that.[4] NUTTERS...

[3] Published in 2005 by Faber and Faber. Read this book!
[4] John Harris again – quoting the *Observer* in *So Now Who Do We Vote For?*, p. 104.

* Or how about the time Tony Blair said, in opposition, that he would never introduce top-up fees? The lying, greasy, shifty two-faced ... ARRRGHH! So now, as well as the loans that had already removed "free" higher education, we have top-up fees. Every expert on higher education knows that charging for university will lead to a fall in the number of poorer students. It's already beginning to happen. So, once again, higher education will become something only the rich can afford – unless you want to get into serious debt before your twenty-second birthday. And let's face it, there are much better ways to earn a fifteen-grand debt – sex, drugs, alcohol, credit cards... It's even worse when you consider that Tony Blair, the posh, privileged public-school git, benefited from the "free" system he is now destroying, as did so many of his generation. God – I want to swear so badly that my eye has just popped out![5]

* And then there are those bastard SATs. Eventually they'll be giving those to babies in the womb, and when they're born, they'll all be separated into "clever", "not so clever", "dumb rich so you're OK", "dumb poor so you're shagged" and "don't even bother just give 'em a fag and Burberry cap and be done

[5] It's OK, I popped it back in (and the word, in case you were wondering, is a lot like Canute with a couple of letters missing and the rest rearranged).

with it" groups for the rest of their sorry little lives...

What about learning because it's *fun*? Reading because it's fun? Just plain fun? Or teaching everyone equally rather than splitting them up into manageable groups like a Blairite SS? When I was at junior school we used to paint fishes and stick tacks into fat kids' bottoms. Now they're all full of angst and stressing about sodding SATs. It's just too American!

That's it – I can't breathe now. Time to move on to...

5 RACISM

This one is dead easy. Racism, as we all know, is stupid. Wrong. Immoral. But *why* is it all of those things?

Well, think about it this way. Racism is all about hating someone or doing things against someone solely because of the colour of their skin. And skin colour is all-important. But which one of us chose the skin we are wearing? None of us were sitting in our mothers' bellies thinking, I know – I'd like to be born black! There isn't some great machine where you can press buttons and decide to be white. The colour we are is an *accident of birth*. And because it's an accident of birth – in other words we don't control it – why get so wound up about it? It just makes no sense.

Lots of people claim not to be racists, but there *must* be a few about in Britain simply based on the number of reported incidents of racial attacks. Here are a few reasons why I believe that racism in the UK isn't dead:

* The shameful reporting of asylum and immigration issues – especially the photos in newspapers that always show black, brown or Eastern European faces. Where are all the white South Africans, Australians, New Zealanders and those damn Yanks?
* You are more likely to be excluded from school if you are a black teenage male than anyone else – at least four times more likely.

* About ten thousand England fans chanted "I'd rather be a Paki than a Turk" and "Die Muslim die" during a game against Turkey in April 2003 and no one at the BBC heard them. Apparently. Funny that – because I was watching and I heard them. Hang your heads...

* *Little Britain* can take the piss out of Asian youths and Thai women using crude stereo-types, but if someone did that with Jewish people it would be called anti-Semitic.

* Because of Stephen Lawrence, Anthony Walker, Shiblu Rahman, Qamir Mirza, the Najeib brothers, Satpal Ram, Rolan Adams, Ricky Reel, Winston Silcott, Mikey Powell, the Romany Gypsy community, Azelle Rodney, Cherry Gross and so many others.[1]

* You are three times more likely to be stopped, searched and arrested if you are Asian than if you are white, and eight times more likely if you are black.

* Black people make up 15.5% of the prison popu-lation yet only 2.8% of the total UK population.[2]

The last two points lead many people to link black people with crime. Like Sir Ian Blair, the head of the Metropolitan Police, who back in 2002 was cited in the *Evening Standard* as saying that most muggers

[1] For more information see the wonderful **www.blink.org.uk** site.
[2] See the websites for the Commission for Racial Equality and Black Britain at **www.cre.gov.uk** and **www.blackbritain.co.uk**.

in London are black. Of course street robbery is more likely to be committed by poor people – and the research proves it. Now, in areas of high black or Asian populations, *they* are more likely to be the poorest. But in cities such as Liverpool or Newcastle the poorest mostly tend to be white. Therefore WHITE people do most of the muggings carried out in Newcastle. Does this make mugging a white crime? No, it bloody well doesn't!

The same is true of Operation Trident, which deals with "black on black" crime. White people carry out the vast majority of crimes committed in the UK; the vast majority of the victims are white people. So can we please have an operation to deal with "white on white" crime? I didn't think so...

Yet it's not only white people who are racists. Consider the brutal murder of Kriss Donald, a white fifteen-year-old from Glasgow in March 2004. His killers were Asian youths and the murder was racially aggravated. And he is not the only white victim of race crime. However, racist attacks on white people are very rare. The same attacks on ethnic minorities are NOT rare. Either way, it's an indication about racism in the UK.

The bottom line with racism is that it's a disease that affects our country. It DOES exist and anyone that tells you differently is a barefaced liar.

6 ASYLUM AND IMMIGRATION

In the last few years, asylum and immigration have become major issues for politicians and the media. That's not to say that they *are* major issues. They're not. But they have been made to look that way. Newspapers like the *Sun*, the *Daily Mail* and the *Express*, and politicians from the Conservatives and the New Conservatives – I mean Labour – have made an issue out of very little, running with scare stories and, in many cases, just outright lies. As a result the average British subject has been led to believe that:

* Britain is swamped with illegal immigrants and asylum seekers.
* Britain is a soft touch compared to other countries, which is why they all come here.
* Britain takes more than its fair share of these people compared to the rest of Europe and the world.
* These asylum seekers and immigrants live like royalty while "real" Britons face housing shortages and fewer benefits.
* Asylum seekers are criminals and even eat the Queen's swans.

But ALL of the above are absolutely untrue or extremely exaggerated. So let's take each issue and find out what the reality is, according to the groups that actually work with them and have these little things which they can call on when questioned – things called FACTS.

* Britain is NOT swamped with asylum seekers and immigrants. In fact, the entire ethnic minority population of the UK is around 8% and that includes people like me who were born and raised in Britain. According to the Refugee Council, in 2003 there were 49,370 asylum applications to Britain compared with nearly 1.4 million overseas workers (people who came here to do jobs we can't fill).[1] Unfortunately, for many bigots anyone with non-white skin is an immigrant or asylum seeker. In fact, many of the people who come to this country are actually from places like Western Europe, Australia and New Zealand. But they are more likely to be white; and, judging by the newspapers, being a white immigrant is fine.

* In a 2003 MORI poll, misinformed respondents thought that the UK took 23% of the world's refugees – nearly one in four. But that just isn't true. The actual amount is around 2.8% of the world total and not even 0.5% of the total UK population.[2] Even in Europe, Britain is only number eleven on the list of countries that take the most refugees.

[1] See "Tell It Like It Is: The Truth About Asylum" at
www.refugeecouncil.org.uk/news/myths/myth001.htm.
[2] See the website for the UN Refugee Agency at **www.unhcr.org.uk**
and follow the links to statistics.

* Asylum seekers do not take up our benefits. Instead they have a separate service, the National Asylum Support Service (NASS), which only gives them *basic* food and shelter. A single adult in 2005 was getting just £38.96 a week, which is *only* 70% of basic income support.

* According to the Refugee Council, in December 2003 around eighty thousand asylum seekers were receiving support from NASS, compared with 15.5 million Britons who were on benefits. This means that asylum seekers were only taking 0.5% of the total welfare given out by the government. When you consider that it is overseas workers who keep organizations like our National Health Service working, that puts things into a proper perspective. According to the Greater London Authority, in 2003 23% of doctors and 47% of nurses in the NHS were born OUTSIDE the UK.

* The Home Office issued a report in 2002 that showed that people born OUTSIDE the UK, including asylum seekers, contribute 10% MORE to the economy than they take out each year: 10% MORE! In 1998/9 that came to an extra £2.6 BILLION.[5]

* I've already dealt with the "eating our swans" lie in **The Media and Politricks** section, but I

[5] These figures are also quoted in "Tell It Like It Is: The Truth About Asylum".

just wanted to repeat it here because it's so disgraceful.

I'm sure there are some of you who are wondering why we should take any asylum seekers, refugees and immigrants in the first place. Well, there are good reasons for this too:

* Immigration is the bedrock of our future economic success. Without immigrants the UK will not be able to compete with the rest of the world. In areas such as Scotland, the north and Wales there are more jobs than there are people willing to do them. And there is a falling birth rate too, which means, although we've got more and more pensioners, we've got fewer people to replace them in the workforce. Fewer workers means less tax, which will mean hard times for ALL of us. It was the same when my mother's generation arrived in Britain to do the jobs that "real" Britons refused to do. Well, someone's got to do them...
* The world's biggest economy – the USA – is built on immigration. Everyone in the USA is descended from immigrants except for the Native Americans.
* The UK signed the 1951 UN Convention Relating to the Status of Refugees and has a duty to take them. When you consider that

the UK, in bombing Afghanistan and Iraq alongside the Yanks, has helped to create thousands of refugees, you can see why it has a burden to bear.

* Asylum seekers, by the way, are refugees who are waiting to see if they will be allowed to stay in the country they have arrived in. Just thought I'd get that in...

* The UK is also committed (rightly in my opinion) to the United Nations Universal Declaration of Human Rights – the very basis of our international law. Article 14 states that:

Everyone has the right to seek and to enjoy in other countries asylum from persecution. [a]

* In my opinion, if multinational companies like McDonald's and Shell are free to move across international borders; and countries with power like the United States and Britain can seemingly do what they like; then poor people fleeing persecution or looking to achieve safety and better lives for their families should be able to seek asylum anywhere.

And that about wraps things up.

[a] The full Declaration of Human Rights can be found at **www.un.org/Overview/rights.html**.

LAST WORD...

Politics can be confusing, but hopefully this guide has taken some of the more complicated edges off. I certainly hope so, because it took long enough to write! The biggest challenge wasn't what to put in – it was what to leave out. There is so much more to all the issues I've covered, but that's where you come in. If there's anything you've read that has made you laugh, cry or break out in a rage, you can read more for yourselves.

And politics is constantly changing too. During the writing of this guide two of the three main parties in Britain have changed their leader. Who knows – by the time it is published, there could be someone else leading New Labour too. Whatever happens, I hope that reading it has been fun and informative at the same time. And I hope too that it has given you a starting point from which to go on and look at other things.

Because politics is NOTHING without ordinary people. Regardless of what politicians say or do, politics in the UK is all about you. So dust off your point of view, sort out the doublespeak and the media bias from the facts, and get involved. In my opinion, most of our politicians and media are letting us down. Maybe it's time for some new ones?

Warmest wishes,

SOME USEFUL WEBSITES

Here's a list of websites that I used during my research. It isn't the complete list – that would have been far too long – but it's a good starting point...

PARLIAMENT AND GOVERNMENT
www.parliament.uk – everything you ever wanted to know about Parliament but were too bored to ask
www.europarl.eu.int – as above but this time for the European Parliament
www.scottish.parliament.uk – Scotland
www.wales.gov.uk – Wales
www.niassembly.gov.uk – Northern Ireland
www.number-10.gov.uk – the prime minister's website. Send him an email...

POLITICAL PARTIES
www.labour.org.uk – guess who?
www.conservatives.com
www.libdems.org.uk
www.snp.org – the Scottish nationalists
www.plaidcymru.org – the Welsh nationalists
www.uup.org – the Ulster Unionists
www.dup.org.uk – the other Ulster Unionists
www.sdlp.ie – the Social Democratic and Labour Party (Northern Ireland)
www.sinnfein.ie – the nationalists in Northern Ireland

OTHER PARTIES

www.greenparty.org.uk
www.swp.org.uk – Socialist Workers' Party
www.independenceuk.org.uk – UKIP
For any other smaller party just type the name into
Google or some other search engine...

ANTI-RACIST

www.stopthebnp.org.uk – a great site full of
information aimed at stopping the BNP
www.searchlightmagazine.com – the long-running
anti-fascist/racist magazine *Searchlight*. A beacon of
light in a shady world
www.yre.org.uk – find out what your European peers
are doing to combat the spread of racism at Youth
Against Racism in Europe
www.blink.org.uk – a valuable resource for looking at
race attack cases and so on
www.cre.gov.uk – the Commission for Racial Equality
www.blackbritain.co.uk – another great resource for
stories

ELECTORAL REFORM AND BASIC KNOWLEDGE

www.electoral-reform.org.uk
www.charter88.org.uk
www.politics.co.uk – a brilliant resource site
www.revision-notes.co.uk – see the great section on
definitions of political ideology
www.bbc.co.uk – good old Auntie Beeb
www.tuc.org.uk – the Trades Union Congress site

THE IRAQ WAR AND HUMAN RIGHTS

www.truthout.org

www.iranchamber.com

www.greenleft.org.au

www.gwu.edu

www.genevaconventions.org

www.unhcr.org.uk

http://pubs.socialistreviewindex.org.uk/sr267/ morgan1.htm – for the article about Senator Riegle and US supplies of chemicals to Saddam Hussein in the 1980s

www.amnesty.org.uk

www.oxfam.org.uk – exactly what it says on the tin

www.hrw.org – Human Rights Watch website

www.liberty-human-rights.org.uk

SELECTED OTHERS

www.un.org – United Nations

www.imf.org – the official site for the International Monetary Fund

www.worldbank.org – the official site for the World Bank

www.globalexchange.org or **www.corpwatch.org** – just two of the sites that tell you about the human misery caused by the IMF/World Bank

www.jubileedebtcampaign.org.uk

www.globalissues.org

www.monbiot.com – the official site of writer and campaigner George Monbiot. It was a great help to me in my research

http://pilger.carlton.com – as above but this time for John Pilger

www.red-star-research.org.uk – unashamedly socialist site with tonnes of stuff about tax-evading big business and so forth

www.thirdworldtraveler.com – great links and articles about the CIA and its disgraceful activities in the name of "liberty" all over the world

www.statewatch.org – another site that gives the CIA and others a good kicking

www.refugeecouncil.org.uk – the FACTS about asylum and immigration

www.medialens.org – catching the media out when they don't do their jobs properly. A great site

www.wikipedia.org – everything about everything. Don't take my word for it – just check it out

www.michaelmoore.com – the official site of the man who hounds the Bush administration. You might also want to check out **www.fahrenheit911.com** for Moore's excellent film *Fahrenheit 9/11* about the war on terror and Iraq – unless you're an American who loves your president, that is

www.truthseeker.co.uk – a DODGY SITE that I came across looking for articles by John Pilger. This site is for those who have a conspiracy theory for everything, including deluded anti-Semites and outright racists. Approach with extreme caution...

MEDIA SITES

There are hundreds of these. Just search for the media outlet you want. I particularly liked:

http://news.bbc.co.uk

www.guardian.co.uk

www.independent.co.uk

although I also looked at loads of others. Check them out...

USEFUL BOOKS

As with the website list, this isn't all the books that I delved into but it does provide a good reading list for the interested and those with a certain bias...

Ian Budge, Ivor Crewe, David McKay and Ken Newton, *The New British Politics* (third edition, Pearson Longman, 2004)

Mark Curtis, *Unpeople: Britain's Secret Human Rights Abuses* (Vintage, 2004)

Robert Eccleshall, Vincent Geoghegan, Richard Jay and Rick Wilford, *Political Ideologies – An Introduction* (Hutchinson, 1986)

Al Franken, *Lies and the Lying Liars Who Tell Them* (Penguin Books, 2004)

John Harris, *So Now Who Do We Vote For?* (Faber and Faber, 2005)

Jack Huberman, *The Bush-Hater's Handbook: An A–Z Guide to the Most Appalling Presidency of the Past 100 Years* (Granta Books, 2004)

John Kampfner, *Blair's Wars* (The Free Press, 2004)

Michael Moore, *Stupid White Men ... and Other Sorry Excuses for the State of the Nation!* (Penguin Books, 2002)

Michael Moore, *Dude, Where's My Country?* (Penguin Books, 2004)

Piers Morgan, *The Insider: The Private Diaries of a Scandalous Decade* (Ebury Press, 2005)

John Pilger, *Hidden Agendas* (Vintage, 1999)

Alan Renwick and Ian Swinburn, *Basic Political Concepts* (second edition, Hutchinson Education, 1987)

Anthony Sampson, *Who Runs This Place?: The Anatomy of Britain in the 21st Century* (John Murray, 2004)

Roger Scruton, *A Dictionary of Political Thought* (Pan, 1983)

There are literally hundreds of other books you can check out. Try the politics section at your local bookshop or library and get reading. It's amazing how much dirt you can dig up if you try...

ACKNOWLEDGEMENTS

With many thanks to:

Burntwood School, Tooting

Djanogly City Academy, Nottingham

Loxford School of Science and Technology, Ilford

Pilton Community College, Barnstaple

BIOGRAPHY

Bali Rai is the author of several teen novels and short stories. Born in 1971 he grew up in Leicester and his working-class, British Asian background influences and grounds his writing. He graduated from Southbank University, London, with a degree in Politics and has a keen interest in current affairs. Bali's debut novel, *(Un)arranged Marriage*, won the Angus Book Award in 2002, and has been followed by further successful novels including *Rani and Sukh* and *The Whisper*, which have firmly established him as a leading voice in teen fiction. His books have been translated into over ten languages.

Bali enjoys cooking, travelling, going to the pub and ranting about New Labour (sometimes he manages to combine the last two). He is also a dedicated Liverpool FC fan. At the moment he's busy writing his new book.